Award recognition for *nîtisânak*

Winner of the 2019 Writers' Trust of Canada
Dayne Ogilvie Prize for LGBTQ Emerging Writers

Winner of the 2019 Quebec Writers' Federation
Concordia University First Book Prize

Shortlisted for the 2019 Quebec Writers' Federation
Mavis Gallant Prize for Non-Fiction

Finalist for the 2019 Indigenous Voices Award for
Published Prose in English

Finalist for the 31st Annual Lambda Literary Award for
Lesbian Memoir/Biography

nîtisânak

WITHDRAWN

nîtisânak

lindsay nixon

METONYMY PRESS

Montreal, QC

First edition
Fourth printing - 2020
Printed and bound in Canada by Imprimerie Gauvin
Illustrations for "For My Descendants" by Kablusiak
Cree language editing by Chelsea Vowel
Editorial consultation from Leanne Betasamosake Simpson
Cover: Photo by Dayna Danger (www.daynadanger.com)
　　　Featured earrings by Savage Rose
　　　Featured necklace by Mad Aunty

Versions of the following chapters have appeared elsewhere:

"wîhtikow," *The Malahat Review* 197, Indigenous Perspectives, Winter 2016.
"Vision 8: pihpihcêw," *Prism* 57.1, Fall 2018.
"Toxic Masculinities," *Room* 39.4, This Body's Map, 2016.
"Prayer 9: For My NDN Bb Girls," in "ndncountry," a special joint issue of *Prairie Fire* and *Contemporary Verse 2*, September 2018.

Portions of this printing of the book were edited to address concerns about the appropriation of African American Vernacular English by Indigenous communities. Thank you to the Black community members in Montreal and Toronto who generously supported the author in dialogue about these edits.

Published by Metonymy Press
PO Box 143 BP Saint Dominique
Montreal, QC H2S 3K6
Canada
metonymypress.com

Library and Archives Canada Cataloguing in Publication

Nixon, Lindsay, 1987-, author
　　　Nîtisânak / Lindsay Nixon.

Issued in print and electronic formats.
ISBN 978-0-9940471-7-5 (softcover).–ISBN 978-0-9940471-8-2 (HTML)

　　　1. Cree Indians--Kinship. 2. Indian gays--Family relationships.
I. Title.

E98.S48N59 2018　　　　306.76'608997323　　　　C2018-903217-0
　　　　　　　　　　　　　　　　　　　　　　　　　　　　　　　　　C2018-903218-9

For mom and nikâwiy

Contents

Love Story Medicine[1]

NDN love: "If we were to trust popular and scholarly representations of Native People we would have to conclude that they,
unlike any other peoples in the world, are without love,"[2] and/or
do you believe in life after NDN love[3]

Is there really such thing as NDN love, as trauma bb love,
as love for the unloved? Or is NDN love just a tall tale I
heard Kenny G and Dolly Parton sing about on the radio
in my grandpa's truck, one dry, hot prairie summer afternoon, sipping the warm pop and eating the Old Dutch
ripple chips he let me get at an isolated gas station a few
towns over, while he worked in his garage?
Islands in the stream
That is what we are.[4]
It's probably just that ~prairie NDN thing~ though. If
love seems unattainable, for us prairie NDNs, it's only because we've lost our sacred connection to the land, and to
all creation. We've lost our ability to speak and be spoken
to by animals.[5] We've lost the intimacy of being.
If love seems impossible, for me and my plains NDN
kin, it's only because they came into our homes in the
middle of the night and stole our babies from their beds.
They shackled them in tiny handcuffs and sent them miles

1

and miles away where they were put into prisons—alone, frightened, hungry, and cold. Some of them never made it home; some of them died trying. The ones who did come back no longer knew tenderness, recoiling at its touch, and passed this static on to the war-torn nerves of my generation.

If love seems hard, on the open prairie, for me and my neechies, it's probably because this world hardened us. Out there, amidst the scarcity feels, we learned that scarcity and depressive affect were the norm, and tenderness and care were not. Someone tricked us—told us that we are competition, and not siblings. That individual voices weaken other individual voices, instead of that our collective voices hold a power that can destabilize nations of yt men.

If love seems hard for us plains NDNs it's because they stole the words out of our mouths, the ones that describe our relationships to one another through action-based intentions, rather than name and claim with nouns—colonial capitalism infected our sacred words.

If love seems hard it's because love is heartbreaking for people like us, like us prairie NDNs. Cynicism and paranoia have made their way into our hearts, begun to fester and eat away at the spirit. Cynicism that manifests as knowledge that the world is a stage wherein we are only allowed to play out our suffering because what is settler colonialism if not one giant trigger for Black, Indigenous, and displaced peoples (and the ultimate gaslight, too[6])? Affect that is always followed by paranoia that "survivance"[7] and "resilience" are just other ways to keep us down—true—and, ergo, we will always be down and out (of love).

But I know that to love still, without pretension, without fear of overt romanticism, and despite that it is hard—well that's our power, annit[8]? At our most essential, we still got love and that *do it for the city,*[9] prairie NDN ~vibe nation~.

To love as delicately as I burn sage, to love as ceremony, to love hard, well, that's where my dominion lies.

The story of Mom and Dad, as told by niya (me), quilted together from stories told to me by adopted kin

My mom met my dad when they were both fourteen at pipe-band, which is exactly as it sounds: a band comprising youth who play bagpipes and drums, march in formation, and travel the world to compete in pipe-band competitions. My mom and dad played the snare drum and bagpipes, respectively, and my dad was actually quite good. He once desired to tour professionally when he was a young idealist, but later in life he would settle on teaching bagpiping, a mid-level engineering job, and a house in a nice neighbourhood with my mom.

They built that suburban, perfectly manicured lawn life my mom had always dreamed of—constructed and built up intentionally as a constant evocation of her upward mobility. "She always had to have the best and the newest and nicest things," my grandma once said to me. My mom formed her home, and her conception of what "home" meant, around capitalist cravings for things and accumulation. While perhaps not the most humble of values, I admit, now that she is gone, having passed away when I was only twenty-eight, commercial smells—The Bay, hotels, and bleached sheets and towels—always remind me of her, and became my home, too. When I was living alone in downtown Regina, sometimes we wouldn't have spoken for weeks, months even. I would loiter through The Bay to comfort myself, trying to surround myself with the feeling of her. Well, sense memory, and to lift a dress or two, when I was on a low budget but had an inherited taste in class mobility.

My mom grew up on the north side with my working-class grandparents—my grandpa at CN and my grandma at a photo development centre, largely leaving my mom to take care of the home. I mention the companies my grandparents worked for because if working-class prairie folk trust in anyone, it's the companies they work for, and their unions. In the prairies, the union, the company, pays your pension, health care, and time off, on top of your wages—not chump change, at all, to my grandparents' generation, who remember when everyone was dirt poor because they lived and worked in small farm communities, and not "big cities" like Regina, Saskatchewan, where I grew up. I would later learn in a 100-level sociology course that the stories my grandparents told about country rule, before the rise of the city, are formally discussed as the mass migration of rural populations to urban municipalities—a sociological phenomenon known as urbanization, or rural to urban migration, resulting from the mechanization of farms and the onset of factory culture. A realization that there's university activism rhetoric, and then there's the streets, the people, because, to me, the folks in my family weren't just a faceless phenomenon. They've lived through industrialization, and they can now tell the stories of its effects on rural communities.

My mom's role in rearing my Auntie D* (her younger sister), keeping their home, and making sure there was a meal on the table at 6 p.m. might raise eyebrows now. But my grandparents grew up during the Depression era when there were clearly defined gender roles on the farm and in the small-town economies of the dirt towns that surrounded them. The "bois" worked the farm, and the "girls" raised the little kids, cooked, and cleaned the house. The punishments were equally real for not falling in line with prairie gender performativity on either side,[10] though—a belt, a slap, or maybe even a beer bottle or boot to the head, depending on how gay the non-observance. For most, *Brokeback Mountain* was just a solid love story. For folks from the prairies, gay panic is naturalized, and queer and trans death on the plains expected.

My mom knew she wanted more for her kids than what she had grown up with, that aforementioned perfectly manicured lawn life. She would tell me that she didn't want to repeat what she experienced as my grandma's icy demeanour and distance from the home, her resistance to hugs and the words "I love you." I always thought my grandma's distance was the result of surviving her dad's farm, country men, droughts, depressions (mental and economic), and days so lean she would eat potatoes for months, in all the ways one could—pierogies, fried for breakfast in a cast iron pan, baked in tinfoil, etc. Still, my mom envisaged home as an aesthetic representation of love; she was an early nurturer of my interest in the aesthetics of intimacy and closeness, though she struggled to express love outside a corrupt, capitalist moment.[11]

My parents' families met through a network of Scottish and British social communities that had developed over a century of settlement in the prairies. They were centralized around small-town churches for my grandparents' generation, and around cultural groups like social clubs, organizations, and pipe-bands for my parents' generation. Ytness on the prairies manifests as simultaneous pride in settler status and immigrant heritage—in the case of my parents' families, as Scottish pride. Romanticized narratives about yt migration to the prairies were a way of keeping community with like people—a yt nationalist commonality in the prairies—built upon the claiming of immigrant status through ancestors and close relatives, and upholding those ancestors' traditions through cultural activities that celebrated "the motherland." It was a polite Canadian kind of racism wherein no one actually says that they are keeping Black, Indigenous, and other people of colour outside of their communities, at least out loud. It just manifests in microaggressions that keep yt communities in the prairies increasingly insular, by socializing around Scottish (or Irish, Italian, and German) clubs and curling rinks that, by their very mandates, keep Black and Indigenous people out under the guise of honouring yt settler histories.

In a different vein, perhaps overidentification with stories of relatives who were fleeing from Europe was a way to claim Canadian nativism as the descendant of someone who had settled the prairies, having run from poverty and persecution in their home country and bravely endured the open prairies for generations. *Our families have survived here for over a hundred years. We are that holy wild wild (prairie) west.* It's a double consciousness that alleviated my yt kin of guilt for the violent removal of Indigenous Peoples from my lands, and perhaps even for the racist affect that continued among the yt settlers. But, I digress. This isn't that story, yet—even though it kind of always is, you know?

This is a love story, and as the story goes, my mom gave my dad a valentine that had Lucy from *Peanuts* on it. The inside of the card read, *Be my valentine or I'll slug ya*, and my dad swooned. It would be an almost perfect summation of their dynamic for the rest of her life. She always ruled our house with a firm hand, and my dad would fall in line. We all would. Though at times respect for her and fear of her blended a little too easily—a dynamic I wouldn't

7

untangle until much later in life.

Like a good prairie boi, in Sask Power my dad did trust. The company prettied his wrist with an expensive watch when he reached twenty-five years of service, when he finished a multi-million-dollar project on a coal mine in my traditional territories. In retrospect, my dad and I were always set up to be in opposition to one another. He had taken his piece of land he was entitled to, had *worked hard* for it, his 180 acres,[12] and I wasn't to breathe a word about how it all went down on my body. But, again, this isn't that story, yet (while it always is).

This is the story of Mom and Dad, high school sweethearts who met at fourteen, who loved each other through decades of transformation and upheaval. Through the lonely prairie winters when my dad travelled for months at a time for his work as project manager on coal plants across Saskatchewan, a job that was no doubt a part of my mom's perfectly calculated life—and my mom lived in the silence. That was her sacrifice for this life she had aspired to: when she saw the double wheel around the moon[13] and knew loneliness in the harsh isolating horizon of a prairie's winter storm.

My mom and dad loved one another through my mom's health issues, when she was diagnosed with von Willebrand disease after giving birth to my brother and almost dying from blood loss. VWD is a rare genetic blood disorder—so rare it would make my mom a research study whenever she entered the hospital. The disease was debilitating to her.

Everything I've read about VWD has indicated that it's not overly harmful, and that its carriers live long and active lives. That's not my experience. My experience of VWD is having to say goodbye to my mom multiple times throughout my youth, in case she didn't "make it," as my dad put it. My experience of VWD is my mom in and out of intensive care for long stints, her first when I was in the fifth grade, with infections her body could not fight off. I remember my mom becoming housebound, hospitalized, and incapacitated so often she could no longer keep her job as a nurse educator. She loved her job deeply. I remember when she broke her femur, a product of being raised just above the poverty line and the lack of calcium in her diet, and her white blood cells attacked the steel plate the doctor had inserted to heal the bone like it was an infection. She was in intensive care for weeks and never fully healed. What she did get, in the hospital, were the pills.

I remember my mom's painkiller addiction, though we never called it that. It's not addiction when it's a yt woman on pharmaceutical opioids—it's just disability. My mom's pill use began as her attempt to cope with the constant sickness and pain, and ended in a thick fog of addiction, wherein she would fall asleep randomly during the day and often be incoherent. One could perhaps argue that it even ended her life, given that what led to her cardiac arrest was an internal bleed that started in her stomach as the result of an ulcer. My mom went into the hospital one night for what began as a stomach ache and ended up dying only hours later because she bled out too quickly and the oxygen wasn't reaching her brain. It seemed like a morbid joke, when I first heard, after everything else she had been through.

The pressure from my mom's illness strained on our family and we began to suffocate in the tension because, though I'm not a waspy yt, I did grow up among them. The silence, the shame, the paranoia—swarming. The tension of the isolated home, behind lock and key, in the nicer neighbourhoods where the cops never look, and your dad can get away with throwing you against a wall by your neck if he wants to, even if you run into the night screaming for someone, anyone, to save you. But this isn't that story, yet. Even if it always kind of is.

This story is about the laughter, humour, and intimacy maintained through decades of doctor's appointments, sleepless nights, and a thousand runs between work, home, and the hospital caring for her. This is a story about all her bouts in intensive care and her long stays in the hospital—afterward changing bandages, supporting her when she walked, and helping her bathe, dress, and perform other essential activities.

This story is about that long love that transcends the present and the teenage passion of a fourteen-year-old's crush. That good love, that so rarely exists. That love I've searched for in my chosen kin, for as long as I've been searching for chosen kin. I mean, just because they couldn't always love me right doesn't mean they didn't teach me a little something about it.

This is the story of teenage lust, of secretly holding hands in the back of the bus, and making a commitment at fourteen years old to put in one day, then another, then another, until all the days added up to a forever. No matter how clichéd that sounds, that's just how it went down. This is the story about love living and surviving through my mom's chronic and irreparable illness, and her inability to have the other children she had manifested her home for; of surviving sadness and grief at her loss of future children, having had to have a hysterectomy, only to find a renewed resolve to be a family, still.

This is a love story, and as the story goes, my mom wrote a letter to social services, enraged. They were a good, Christian family, weren't they? How dare they put her and my dad under such scrutiny. Weren't they worthy of a family, at least more worthy than some of those foster parents who had adoptable kids in their homes? She would tell the story beaming, a satisfied smile across her face. It was so clear to her that her letter secured me to their home, because only a few months later, they would get me. The way my mom tells it, she had been pouring labour into creating our family for years, and this was her last chance.

The story of nikâwiy and nindede, woven together from stories told to me by blood kin, or who's to say what's lies and what's The Truth

Of course, there are two sides to every story, and the second portion of this one begins with nindede and nikâwiy (my Cree mom).

This story is made understandable through a warning. In the prairies, The Truth is a yt man. The Truth is whatever the yt man says, and whatever truth is said by the yt man is the ruling law of the *holy wild wild (prairie) west*. This story is made understandable by the admittance that when I listen to nikâwiy talk about her life, I've often wondered if she's lying—where her (our) truth lies. I've told people, nikâwiy isn't lucid, you see, I don't know what's lies and what's the truth. Ergo, I've told people, nikâwiy is just another crazy squaw; I'm just another crazy squaw. As if the real world doesn't integrate with the otherworldly for us Cree people. As if the whole prairie world isn't the ultimate gaslight to someone like nikâwiy, designed to make her feel crazy when she contends that perhaps her disappearance, her spiritual destruction, wasn't warranted. As if truth isn't relative and, if she contends that her experience is true, well then, isn't it, to her, at least?

I always felt like my dad was keeping something from me about my adoption, but I could never identify what. When I turned eighteen and pulled my papers, I realized that it was likely that I was millennial scooped. If I told my dad this, he would probably say, That's not the truth. I say, I have no adoption papers, only an admittance to foster care and a court order from my mom and dad to petition to adopt me. They found me in foster care and the courts convinced nikâwiy to sign the papers on me. I was adoptable, with squishy Cree cheeks, to boot. But these are the things you don't talk about: not in adoptee organizing that centres sixties scoopers, not to one of the most dangerous yts out there—yt lady social worker—who could bring trouble into your home, and certainly not to your yt parents.

All this begs the question, whose truth do we privilege as The Truth, in the story of nikâwiy and nindede? This story is made understandable by my assertion that nindede doesn't get a name—not father, not dad, and not even sperm donor. Nookomis (my Saulteaux grandma) says we don't say their names anymore, the men who chased us off the rez, terrorized us in the cities, and made us their emotional surrogates. I have always been caretaking beyond my capacity for the men in my life. For sexually abusive nindede who constantly reaches out, weasels his way around blocked numbers and profiles, wanting to "heal" me and my siblings, when he really just wants to get into our heads and fuck with us some more. For my brothers who are quick to anger and despise the way my face curves in the same way nikâwiy's does because it represents the love she could never give. So I take care of them, let them stay with me for free, buy them food, give them shelter, and listen to them talk about the woman they left behind in shambles, having made off with whatever money she had in her purse and what fit in a backpack. And, when I no longer do, then, of course, I'm a bitch, or so they say when they call from a payphone downtown just to let me know that if they kill themselves, it's my fault—this is the mess my father and older generations of men in my family left in the wake of their terror.

Uncles, dads, and grandfathers, except stripped of their titles. I don't know if giving nindede kinship is much better—but I have to call him something and, at the end of time, he'll always be my Saulteaux kin and the head of my clan. We can pretend that I have power over him in refusing his name, or we can accept the power he exercises over me within the dystopian now,[14] now that our kinship lines are sick with patriarchy. His unnaming is more of an unclaiming, anyway.

Other neechies will often ask me why I claim nookomis from Coté who married into the Ironstands of Tootinaowaziibeeng, and indebted us to this patrilineal lineage forevermore, and not my dad, even though he still lives on the rez—usually rez NDNs with sôniyâwak, or money, when they're trying to place me. The placing of me by rez NDNs is always carefully considered, or more accurately judged, by the rez I'm registered to. Of course, the rez I am registered to is a legal, and perhaps patrilineal-turned-masculinist, designation that was given to me by colonial legislators with no capacity to understand the fluidity of Cree, Métis, and Saulteaux identity within my community, and the kinship-based ways we shared lands—who sought only to number, categorize, and manage our bodies. My identity is never understood by rez NDNs who try to place me in terms of who loves me and claims kinship with me, as nookomis has taught me—the feminine and relational ways of understanding where I belong in this world. As nookomis has said, You (I) can never forget that you're (I'm) Cree-Métis, too—*first*. Tl;dr: Kinship is the original and most important form of Indigenous law and governance. Fuck the treaties.

But there's a little more to this question of where I'm from: the rez NDNs want to know if my people are those medium-poor NDNs from the rez, or maybe even some nouveau riche neoliberal upwardly mobile neechies from the rez, with ties to casino money or a money-laundering chief somewhere in the mix. Sorry to disappoint, we're those dirt-poor ones from the city, who the NDN bro assholes would beat up when we came to stay with our granddad for a while.

NDNs just want to be the fanciest, to suss out the *bad* families. An NDN will spend a lifetime making a name critiquing the state, only to turn around and be one of those what's-his-dollar-value-per-square-mile, looking-for-the-*good*-family-lines-in-your-family-names, give-their-name-to-any-colonial-machine-that'll-lift-it-up-and-pay neechies. Honestly, fuck the rez—our little plots of land KKKanada gave us to squabble over, to distract us. I'm honestly supposed to believe a rez like Kahnawake is *très refusal* because it's a self-functioning community that resists amalgamation under the state, when it's putting up eviction notices on its women's doors, and addicts are dying in its darkest corners because stigma about drug use and alcohol pushes them into unsafe situations. That's cool, K-Town—keep destroying one another over that little plot of land that the man gave you, calling it the holy land while dictating what NDNs are good enough to swim in your bourgeois waters, as if you could own the waters to begin with. Much teachings. Very tradish.

The rez ain't so pure. The women, gender-variant, and sexually diverse kin in my family fled rape and unspeakable abuse on the rez, another poorly funded, forgotten prairie rez with zero resources to sell out on, as early as they could and can only go back in groups now, and only as necessary to get payouts. How could you return to the place where your abusive dad's uncle is the preacher, and his cousin is running for chief and council—a nation ruled by men who are the lifeblood of my terror of a granddad? How could you return to a place where, if you entered alone, without the support of your male kin, rape and violence against you would almost be certain? Where, if you were lucky enough to be blessed with housing, which, on Toot, consists of a broken-down trailer in a field, it would likely be broken into and burned down by community members who knew you were an easy target? The treaty left its mark on our bodies, and then named us all after our Saulteaux male relatives we were trying to escape. But don't underestimate me by erasing this prairie hardness. There are multiple ways to warrior up, one such way being getting on toward those flashing city lights (*iskwêwak, iskwêwak, get that sôniyâwak*[15]).

The fancy rez NDNs tell ghost stories to scare one another. My family tells ghost stories to shield us from the truth by creating a protective barrier of lies—a mysterious skin.[16] nikâwiy is from Prince Albert, but has been living in the east end of Saskatoon since her early twenties. nohkom was in residential schools and married a yt man and moved to the city shortly thereafter. Much like nohkom, nikâwiy has never said my granddad's name to me. While I don't know much about what happened in that house, during nikâwiy's youth, I do know that the women who resided there left in pieces. nohkom has been a non-verbal shit disturber, a term I use with absolute respect and admiration, and more specifically completely snowed 24/7, for years. She has never been able to speak with clarity about where she came from or what her community before moving to the city might have been, preferring instead the "hiding in plain view" project of her generation of Cree-Métis women who made their way into prairie cities. Regardless of what the yt witchy queers say, we, the prairie NDN fems, were the ones born to the witches the yt men didn't burn, born to our moms in the bellies of the small cities they ran to. Don't tell me that we ain't treaty people too, when the treaty cut right through us.

My focus on my matrilineal lines of descent doesn't indicate that I devalue Métis, Anishinaabe, and Cree kinship teachings that envisage men as an essential part of a balanced community. Instead, my intent is to acknowledge the insidious colonial masculinities that have poisoned my patrilineal lines, turning many of my men kin from reciprocal relations into perpetrators of harm, and to describe the parts of my family's identity that cannot be restrained by colonial law and categorizations of our communities. Tl;dr: the yt men in my family came looking for victims, and the Native men took what was left.

The only occupation I've known nindede to have had is what I've heard called lovingly "a man about town." In plainer terms, he owned a strip club in Prince Albert that was actually a drug front. Needless to say, he was always in and out of jail. Not needless because of his involvement with petty crime, but because everything he touched turned to ash. I wish it were just petty crime. Somehow that's easier to name. That's strategic. That's about a countercultural fucking way of being—the original way of being of these territories. What's harder to name, and to wrap my mind around, are the sex charges.

nikâwiy still can't believe she and my brothers survived that house and survived nindede. Whatever The Truth is about my family is now an amalgamation of my mom's assimilationist values, my dad's authoritative Truth, and nikâwiy's breaks from reality. What I do know is that nikâwiy was on the receiving end of some of the most terrifying abuse of her life, even after my granddad had left his mark. My health was in peril. She needed to put me in foster care, just for a little bit, where they could take care of me. I'd come back, she told herself. Just like my brothers, who they let come back all the other times. But this time, I didn't come back.

Don't mistake my words for trauma porn, because this is just how it went down for us. If these stories can't be told without a yt tear being shed, that's not my problem. No, my trauma is not a commodity, but my story doesn't always have to be uplifting, resurgent, or revolutionary to be my truth, either.

Toxic Masculinities

Nindede

Nindede was the first man that ever hurt me. While I've always cared gently for my rambling heart, I've also wondered if this was a quality of nindede embodied through me. Nindede ran from every wigwam and every woman he ever laid with, leaving a trail of fatherless children across the prairie. While his absence was felt, so was his presence. I can still see the obscurity in nikâwiy's face when he is mentioned. I feel his shadow dimming the spirit of my siblings. I will never fully know what happened to put me in the hospital, to make nikâwiy sign my adoption papers. What I do know is gratitude toward a mom's love, rows and rows of tobacco flowers blooming in the dark, and my first lesson in toxic masculinities: that any man, no matter how close to me, can, and will, hurt me.

niya

When the stranger bumps his shoulder into me, hard, without an ounce of concern, I can feel the fire bubbling inside of me. The heat from the concrete rising up, through my feet, reverberating like electricity about to erupt magma through every orifice of my body. Lava that will oxidize every atom and molecule of his body on contact. The city as embodied trauma. The trauma of settlement. I spin around to yell after him, letting the anger fully consume my spirit as it has so many times before. I don't know where the empowerment ends and the dissolution begins anymore.

Terra Nullius

It's "Easter Sunday" in Penobscot, Passamaquoddy, and Abenaki territories. Driving through the peninsula I get to meet the cracked earth wetlands of these territories. I get to spend time with my relation, kihcikamiy, the ocean, compelling me with all its awe-inspiring beauty and power. Earlier in the day we eat lobster, another gift from kihcikamiy and nîkihcikihik (my big parent, here a gender-neutral way of referring to nature). While I am humbled and grounded, and feel both gratitude and love for nîkihcikihik, an angst roars inside of me—just like the roaring waves of kihcikamiy. I feel a loss for the teachings of these territories and the relations whose stories I don't know, whose words haven't reached me. There has been an interruption in our kinship, our ways of sharing love as relations and love for our mutual relations, like kihcikamiy. A way of being and knowing that was replaced by a system reliant on the destruction and sickening of land, the destruction of our kinships. Toxic masculinities that have bled into the earth and disrupted our relationships to the land.

Blood Quantum and Borders

"What's your percentage?" the border guard asks.

"I don't know. We don't really do it that way in KKKanada," I respond.

He looks at my status card and then back at me with disdain. I've called his bluff. "So, you're an American Indian then?" he asks.

"I'm Anishinaabe and nêhiyaw..."

"It doesn't matter, it's the same thing! Look, next time you better know your percentage. I can't let you across this border unless you're fifty percent," he says, as he bends over to peer into the car menacingly. I feel my whole body stiffen and I turn my gaze forward. I remember the starlight tours. And officer 3191. I've heard the stories about when they arrested Kahn-Tineta at the border for refusing to claim Canadian or American citizenship, claiming instead Wolf Clan. What they did to her when they detained her. What the wîhtikow could do to me knowing I have disappearance in my blood. I feel a thunder inside, rumbling, trying to escape through my throat, stinging my nose hairs, reverberating my vocal chords, beckoning me to speak. I want to cite the Jay Treaty, remind him that he can't prevent me from crossing his colonial borders by land because these are my territories. I've exposed an uncomfortable truth for him—that these borders are illusory. That, perhaps, his power is too.

Instead I reply, "Oh, I didn't know that. I'll be sure to figure that out once I'm back home. Thanks for letting me know." I almost choke on the words as they escape my mouth, leaving a burning sensation in my chest.

They did an unnatural thing when the settled their homes here, when they traced and cut these borders through my body. My flesh, an offering, a reminder that I must always be dying.

Rape Culture

The toxic masculinity that is hardest to name is "not rape." Probably because it exists within a space that isn't real. Because "not rape" is never meant to be spoken about, I can only speak from my own experiences of what it might be, even if I'm probably a fucking liar. To me, "not rape" is never feeling pleasure from sex until my early twenties, though I had been promiscuous since my teens, because no one told me about my clit and, inevitably, no one had told the dudes I had been fucking either. "Not rape" is letting him slither his hands slowly, slowly, slowly downward just after offering, As long as you're not an Indian, referencing my racial ambiguity. It's every boi I've ever kissed who, when I pulled away, pulled me closer and said, C'mon, baby. "Not rape" is every parent who tells their daughters, When he hits you that means he likes you, sweety, and their sons, If she doesn't warm up to you at first, just keep trying! You're a nice guy!

Dad

The world told my dad that the emotions of yt men are objective, logical, and reasoned. In contrast, I was not. I was not yt, not a man; not objective, not logical, nor reasoned. I was other. I am silent when he calls, not wanting to stir our already simmering relationship. I listen while he berates me, without provocation, as if my existence is an affront to his very being.

He tells me that Islamic peoples are inherently violent, by virtue of some small percentage of them being "extremists." I know he's trying to provoke me and repeat a communication cycle we've found ourselves in many other times wherein we escalate into violent words and actions. I struggle not to respond, choosing to make it through this one interaction without a fight. I know I am complicit in Islamophobia, in doing so. If you ask me, Christianity is the most brutal religion because of it having been utilized as a colonizing logic for appalling things Christians did in residential schools, and for centuries to marginalized peoples across the globe. Things they got away with, too, in the territories where my dad now resides. He tells me that Indians were at war before settlers arrived here, anyway; it wasn't all kumbaya. He laughs when I go off, when I take the bait. I have to be wrong for him to be right, for him to assert his ultimate Truth.

Maybe my queer, brown body, that has never played by his rules, *is* an affront to his very being. I slacked off and disrespected the forty-hour workweek, making a mockery of his work ethic because my work ethic looks a lot different than his. Though we differ on our definition of ethic because he's more of an Ayn Rand kind of guy. My work ethic looks more like partying, fucking, and fucking around, in service of my heart and my art. His work ethic isn't a work ethic, if mine is. All the work he put into a punishing respect for law, authority, and the company would not have succeeded if he shared my vision of right and wrong.

I'm a *bad girl.* I party, get high, and fuck a little too much. Worse still, I exhibit no remorse or guilt for doing so. But I've always felt those rambling ways in my soul, like there was *nothing like living in a bottle,*[1] like I needed the electricity of the (queer) twilight to bring these tired nerves to life; to remind myself it's worth being alive; to make me feel it all.[2] And I've always known in my heart, even if my parents tried to instill fear in me of using and people who use, of fucking and people who fuck, of other racialized peoples, that even poor brown users, poor brown sex workers, deserve some fucking respect in this post-apocalyptic world. Post-apocalyptic because NDNs have already witnessed the end of their ways of living, being, and loving, and the imposition of a destructive, extractive, and dying world.

If I were okay, not a victim, proudly an NDN, proudly a high gay NDN who loves to fuck multiple people at once, successful despite my loose morals and inability to reform myself, I would disprove The Truth that my dad's psyche and ego were built upon. And what is the prairie home if not a space to nurture and care for the male ego, the working man, the farmer, the factory stooge, making a dime for his family, day in and day out, in noble quiet.

But the necessity of my wrong-ness is about more than my dad's individual authority—it's about moral order on the prairies, too. There are racial scripts encoded in the ways we interact. My dad needed me to believe in The Truth, or else his own moral reasoning around race, his reasoning for my adoption, that I would be better off with a yt family, would be untrue. In retrospect, we were always in opposition, and that's probably why I ran the minute I could. *How can you stay when your heart says no?*[3] Did my heart say no because it's unnatural for me to be still and not in migration, or because it was so misunderstood? Can my dad ever truly love me, like decolonially love me, the way my tired spirit deserves? What is corrupt love other than obligation[4]?

How long was my mom doing emotional labour with my dad, quieting him when he wanted to bring his ego to the table with me, checking his anger so I didn't have to, as I am now? How long was she doing that labour with me, for him? All those years before moving onto another physical plane. In this way I speak to her through the cosmos. She is gone but her spirit lingers, when I can connect with the shadows she left in my world. Would I be so quiet if she weren't gone? My mom deserves some fucking dignity, too. The nurturing spirit ascribed to women on the prairies, made to balance the sting of a hard prairie masculinity, was part of my mother's quiet dignity.

You can tell me the fem/masc, bottom/top rhetoric is so passé in these, the high holy days of gender fluidity. Yes, emotionality and empathic abilities have obligated me to the men in my families. But I still remember when femininity was something that I learned from my mother to nurture and revere. Something that is beautiful.

The Straight Man's Gaze, or Katy Perry[5] Perpetuates a Culture of Violence toward Queer Folks

Why do straight men think that lesbians are just dying to have a three way with them? That kisses and meaningful glances between women are somehow about men, and it's okay to approach lesbian partners on the street and hit on them; that it's not harassment, it's just giving it the ol' college try and/or a game of odds. Why do straight men imagine that lesbian pleasure, desire, and orgasms are by some stretch of the imagination about male sexuality, meant to be performed for their erotic fascination?

> VISION 1: We drop acid at Hotel Saskatchewan, where my mom used to take me for high tea when I was a little girl to teach me the customs of refined yt femininity, and to show me love. Now, in the penthouse suite, I undo those customs one tab of acid and queer orgasm, the kind that floods a bed, at a time. I jump on the bed wearing a cat mask, telling my partner how everything comes from nature, in the midst of a brief stint as a moralist vegan, I'm embarrassed to say, wondering why people prefer processed foods when something as perfect as a grape exists. My partner says the tie on the back of my dress is dangling down so it looks like a cat tail. I get wet when they make me feel cute. We are completely in the moment, and in love.

But somehow, their ex-boyfriend who is partying with us, a current friend who always gave me weird vibes, who stared a little too long, acted a little too possessive over them, still, thinks it's all for him. He had faded away during our moment and now somehow has reappeared with his dick in his hand. I start crying. My partner says, "Oh my God, don't look," covering my face and drawing me close to them. Eventually, once we recover from the shock, we force him out of the room by convincing him that we're going to call security or the cops if he doesn't get out. A reminder that men will only retreat their advances when confronted with the threat of another man. My partner spends the rest of the night crying and rocking back and forth in the bath, trying to wash away the high. Men have already taken so much from us, it should come as no surprise that they would want to take this moment, too.

Skyler

I think that I've been meme-ified because when I get mad I can only think in sassy quips. Tfw you wake up from an anger nap and you still hate the sight of your yt lover's face. Tfw you've been emotionally overextending yourself for yt mascs for the better part of a decade and you don't know if you can do it anymore.

There are so many yt mascs who have left their mark—every time "he" touched me left a mark.[6] "He" is a single yt masc made through an amalgamation of all the bois who have ever marked me. Let's call him Skyler. When Skyler asks, Who is offering safe spaces for trans-masculine people to express their feelings? I think, *LOL, bitch, who is offering that to me?* Excuse me if there's a little sass in my tone but my aunties taught me not to take shit.

It's not that I disrespect trans masculinities or that I'm frivolously claiming that trans masculinities can be homogenized into a universal experience. Rather, I have been subject to the pitfalls of fem binarization to trans masculinities my whole queer life, and the cycles that can emerge from the reification of masculinities that are misogynist, and therefore toxic, even in queer communities. A toxic trans bro is still a toxic bro. And I've met my fair share of toxic bros.

Like with any other form of toxic masculinity, there's a difference between the consciousness-raised, tender trans masculinities, and trans masculinities that reinforce dangerous colonial scripts that make me as their other. Toxic trans masculinities are when Skyler watches my actions with a fine-tooth comb, secretly reading all my emails and texts—but then stays out all night with some young thing, only to return the next morning and tell me, It just made me realize how much I love you, baby. And the emotional overextension that comes when, instead of leaving, I end up processing with him and consoling him for the next four hours, while he's crying in my lap, after having not slept the night before, too worried about where he was.

Toxic trans masculinities are when Skyler shows off in public by treating me like his property, wrapping his arm around my neck and pulling me close in that specific way that peacocks to the rest of the world that this is his pussy. I can tell my "fem presentation" turns him on; see also: the ways my dress and mannerisms signal yt colonial femininities to all those who perceive me and us together, thereby bolstering his gender presentation as well. The emotional capacity ascribed to fem folks kicks in when I wonder if I should say something, if I should tell Skyler I'm uncomfortable with this gesture, but instead I self-modify and stop myself. Make myself encouraging, tender, and affirming to him. I'm afraid I'll illegitimize Skyler's gender. I'm ever unsure about how I feel about our unspoken fem/masc dynamic, and the little gender games he plays, knowing that Skyler never asked me how femininity fits into my gender in the first place.

But I wonder if when Skyler touches me, the lines he traces across my flesh are borders he cuts through me. The same way his ancestors put a border through my territories separating my kin from their homelands—mid-migration in a hunting camp occupying an empty prairie field—away from our lakes, away from our rice, and away from our spirits. Does Skyler consider, when he forces my face into the pillow and calls me a slut, that he evokes

centuries of genocide? Because though I love Skyler inti-
mately and call him family, and though we both find this
game hot, I hope he at least considers what his body pushing into mine means.

Does Skyler know the way his gender invades mine,
the same way the Smithsonian invaded We'wha and a
thousand more settlers will invade her forevermore using
her image as a sterile, anthropological analysis of the traditional genders of my peoples? They witness her power
with a voyeuristic fascination for this dying breed, this so-
called Zuni man-woman, completely separated from their
own complicity in the disappearance of my true spirit.
Genocide of my flesh. I can still feel the conquistadors'
dogs biting into me.

Toxic trans masculinities are Skyler putting me in
danger with police because he takes up too much space:
getting pulled over multiple times for running a red light
while smoking weed in the car, or going 130 while passing
a highway cop right after we had smoked, and still having
the audacity to tell me it isn't his fault. His comfort is primary. It's okay to react in anger toward people who wield
institutional power, like cops, to melt down, and insist that
he was in the right, instead of attempting to identify and
process an emotion. When we arrive home after being in-
terrogated, I cry hysterically in the bathroom, reciting
Bukowski. An asshole, I know, but for some reason he's
the first person who came to my mind, probably ingrained
from the copy of War All the Time that I read so many times
as a nihilist teenager that the spine broke. There are worse
things than being alone.[7] There are worse things than being alone. There are worse things than being alone.

Skyler and I fight the most when I have to explain "taking up too much space" to him, what I mean when I say,

"You're just so yt," when we are talking about his relationship to police officers. Completely unconstructive, I know, but I wasn't in my most empathetic space having just been harassed by the cops who menacingly questioned us because we smelled like weed.

I must've told him a million times that when he drives aggressively it scares me, and then the cops pulled us over and harassed us, just as I feared. Because he doesn't know what it's like to get fucked with by a cop in the middle of the night in a deserted Edmonton street. A cop could make you disappear, like really disappear, and maybe no one would care. Let me correct myself: a cop could make me disappear, and maybe no one would care.

I hold my tongue the time we see the security guard following us in his van when we stop at a park to find somewhere to smoke weed on 420. It's the day after my birthday and we drive around ironically looking at the mansions in the rich neighbourhood, wondering how many million each house costs, and who the Indigenous Peoples of those territories were who were displaced by this richest of settlements. Skyler tells me I'm being paranoid.

VISION 2: Only a few minutes later Coyote stops at our car and looks me in the eyes. I open my window to call out to him. Suddenly, lights come on behind us. I realize the security guard has crept into the parking lot to observe us. He tries to trap us in the parking lot as we drive away. Coyote knows to run away. I feel dark and heavy because if Skyler had only believed me, if we had only moved the car when I had gotten "paranoid," we would have never gotten fucked with by the park narcs.

Why was Coyote there? To warn me? To make sure I knew that Skyler will never understand that Coyote and I are wild things? He forgets that when he and I smoke in public, I'll always be visible, racialized, and vulnerable. I might be a strong-ass NDN but sometimes he needs to protect me, too.

But toxic yt trans masculinities aren't perpetuated solely by lovers, either. Toxic trans masculinities are every masc who has erased my experience to interject his own, every masc who uses his gender to evade accountability for his shitty behaviours, and every trans boi who uses their desirability for social traction, but also to be an unaccountable relation—to duck out on processing and care, and return only when it's most convenient. Toxic trans masculinities are the t-bois club, the lift bros, the I-can't-identify-or-process-an-emotion-and-therefore-have-shitty-communication, the chest-surgery-pics-or-your-transition-isn't-real d00ds, too. Toxic trans masculinities are trying to talk about tender and decolonized masculinities with trans-masc folks, only to have it derailed every ten minutes to talk about ~chest surgeries, brah~. This is when I know I don't fit. That "trans," in its very nature, denotes a physical transition, a medicalized, western vision of trans identity, that erases the multiple genders that have existed in these territories for, like, ever, and the ways Indigenous Peoples often refuse the medical model as a way of validating their genders, just as they refuse all colonial imposition. Toxic trans masculinities are a colonizing logic.

I admit, I fantasize about brown love, brown queer/trans, queer-trans community. Native love. I'm told it exists. That some of us trauma bbs made our way down paths of healing and learned to love our bodies back to life.

Native men aren't such a prize, either. Toxic masculinity knows no bounds.

Imperialism

It was Leanne Simpson who said that sovereignty starts at home[8]—I know this about colonizers too. I used to work as a nanny for two sons, four and six years old, of a British beauty mogul journalist in Brighton. It was also loosely my first job in the publishing industry because sometimes she'd get me to do assistant work for her, mostly calling around to get her beauty samples for her best-of list. The mogul never saw her kids. She would leave early, or stay holed up in her room, all day. I would take the kids to school, pick them up from school, feed them dinner, and put them to bed. Sometimes the beauty mogul would say goodnight to the bois before going out for the rest of the evening. But, for the most part, I was raising these children. That's how those tricky imperialists get you to stay for ridiculously low wages: you begin to feel responsible to the kids. I had become their surrogate mom. The year I worked for them, the mogul forgot to throw the eldest a birthday party, and I paid for a gift for him out of my meagre wages, just so he could feel special that day. But I'm sure the bois look back now and imagine my love wasn't real because I was getting paid to give it.

This is how colonizers are bred, away from their moms, detached from love, and raised by brown women from the colonies, taught to despise their very existence because it is innately connected with the absence of their mothers' love. Taught that, ultimately, we are their imperial labour force.

Sadness Is My Boyfriend[9]

When a friend tells me that DD is a millionaire now, having gotten rich off of bitcoin, the neechie in me thinks, *Damn, I should've had that dude's baby.* The thought makes me laugh because that was exactly what he had always accused me of.

I should have known that he was an asshole when he told me his favourite song was Kanye West's "Gold Digger." Not that Kanye West is inherently a creep (or that he hasn't been a creep, for that matter). But Kanye West in the hands of a yt man ... well, that's another thing altogether. Or maybe the fact that we began flirting while he was still with his longtime live-in girlfriend should have tipped me off. I was just coming off of that addictive, toxic love, where they take your spirit with them and leave your ethics in a total mess—muddled by the ego of an early twenty-something trying to forge an identity of their own. It wasn't my proudest moment.

DD was my overcorrection, my "supposed to be better than the last asshole I was with." But I quickly learned that a steady income doesn't necessarily make a "good guy," no matter what capitalism and your mom's hand-me-down cold war era rhetoric says. He was my lesson that an asshole with a nice apartment, who pays his bills and for expensive dinners, is *still* an asshole.

When I told DD I was pregnant, he said a more paranoid man would think I was trying to trap him. We broke up a week later. I remember his cruelty that day, and the day of my abortion when he came to my apartment and

leaned in to kiss me—now that I had dealt with "the problem." When he did, I understood why they ask you four
different ways in the pre-abortion interview: Is this your
choice? Is anyone forcing you to have an abortion? Did
anyone coerce you to come here today? Do you want an
abortion?

After I denied him, he settled on stalking and intim-
idating me on social media, irate about the men he assumed I was now giving my loving to, promising it would
be different this time. *Sorry*, I'd think. *I already learned that
lesson with the last one.* I felt like I had been tricked. I had
been special ordering *Bitch* magazine and Bikini Kill CDs
to my hometown since I was sixteen. I had been thinking
about feminism, identifying with feminism as a central
tenet of my selfhood, for a minute. Yet, here I was, one of
those mythical girls who got *tricked* into having an abortion. Funny, wasn't it me whose motives were questioned,
who was portrayed as the deceiver, as seeking out his seed
for my own agenda?

In the prairies, The Truth is a yt man. The Truth is
whatever the yt man says, and whatever truth is said by the
yt man is the ruling law of the *holy wild wild (prairie) west.*

My Sexuality

My sexuality, or rather the sexualization of me, has made toxic masculinities ever known to me, a naturalized part of being in the world and perceived as a Native girl. My sexuality is a constant that I am never allowed to forget. And it's always my fault. My body grew breasts, hips, and fatty folds—curves, as postured folks say—from a young age. It betrayed me. I know how high a percentage of men are sexual predators because of the behaviours I could not escape from a young age. When people ask me why my pronouns (correction, when yt people ask me why my pronouns) aren't the most important to me now, I explain that my gender—something I associate very closely with my indigeneity, and lineages of diverse gender in my community—could never be affirmed through the use of colonial language, through one word. I just wish I had the Cree words to say what my traditional gender role is. Though I still appreciate the use of "they" by savvy folks who really *see* me. But, secondarily, when I talk about my gender fluidity now, it's hard to disconnect dysphoric gender embodiment from trauma associated with my body being feminized and sexualized from a young age. Men never let me forget that they see me as a woman, a woman they want to fuck.

My sexuality, first experienced as the sexualization of me, is inappropriate glances and advances from older men who I was supposed to trust, when I was only a minor. All the men who knew I was an easy victim, who knew girls like me were—not easily believed against the word of a doctor, teacher, preacher, or social worker.

Then there were the teachers and community members who sexualized me, afraid that my childhood curiosity would infect their impressionable young yt men. Like the teacher who caught me writing hearts in my notebook with a classmate's name and got my principal to call me out of class because I was in trouble for doing something every young girl would do. Because the very suggestion of my youthful sexuality was a danger to the impressionable yt bois around me.

My sexuality, my presumed Native womanhood, my inherent wildness, was a danger to me and the yt people in my community.

My dad taught me to be afraid of rape, showing me the opening for *A Time to Kill* as a scare tactic, because being a brown girl meant always being in danger of abuse, murder even. As brown girls, it's our duty to protect ourselves from rape—to not go outside late at night, walk to a friend's house alone, or wear provocative clothing. The answer is always to make ourselves smaller, instead of telling bois they shouldn't rape, and calling them in when they harass young girls. When I told my dad that I had been harassed and sexually assaulted in grade school, he responded by asking if the bois who did it were drunk. I admitted they were. "They didn't know what they were doing," he said. I should always be afraid of rape, he was saying, because a rape committed by an affluent yt man or boi is "not rape."

In the prairies, The Truth is a yt man. The Truth is whatever the yt man says, and whatever truth is said by the yt man is the ruling law of the *holy wild wild (prairie) west*.

Running

Creator knows I haven't been perfect, either. But if I feel a boi playing me, believe I am doing it more, faster, and bigger. I will create a distance between him and myself so empty that he won't ever remember what it's like to whisper my name in the dark.

That boi better not force me to speak when I'm mad because I'll tell him to leave or I'll burst out that door like a paskwâwi-mostos thundering across the plains. I'll never stop running. I'll run across countless barstools, through back alleys and strange beds. I'll drown the loss of him with barrels of fire water, dates, and purple haze because I'd rather be without him, and a tragic mess, than a tragic mess because I'm with him.

I'll be just like nookomis. "I didn't know where I was going ... we just took the car and ran," she said to me once about breaking out of the rez. She was only fourteen then. She stole a car with her best friend. They hit the road, westbound—a classic Thelma and Louise situation, except the Native version. A Verna and Erin-Marie situation? Anyway, it was better than hitching a ride. Everyone knew that girls go missing on dirt roads in rural southeastern Manitoba, only a few miles from where those yt bois took Helen Betty Osborne. Except neither of them knew how to drive so they drove the car into a ditch. Nookomis would chuckle when she told me that story, and nonchalantly say, "Yeah, we spent a little time in the lock-up." Locked down or not, my grandma was out. She was gone, running on the plains. I've got running in this here Red River blood. Creator knows this started long before me.

Dear NDN Bro,

You'll never convince me that I'm a liar. That they're liars. That it didn't happen. That you can sue it away. I know because it happened, it's happening, and it will continue to happen, to me. I know because, afterward, the aunties told me how it happened to them. And Ngahiraka told me, "When a rabid dog is running at you, you don't run away. You run straight at it."

Very Best,
Ungrateful, Traitorous, Troublesome Bitch

Bitch

I'm not such a man-hater. It's just that riot grrrl raised me, I'm rigorous as all hell, and I breathe the fire of nookomis into everything I do.

The Prairie Wind Is Gay Af

I'm told that the nature poem is so passé, much too cliché for us city NDNs to write. Fuck that. The prairie wind is gay af.

Books have been written about the prairie wind. It rules everything it touches. It's God.[1] Autumn's warm flurry of whirlwinds around the head, making a conundrum of dry air and messing hair into eyes, brings with it smells and associated memories that will always be my home: sweetgrass, firewood, and hay. But that sweet hot wind of late September that matches my most restless thoughts, which I project on the rolling hills—a wavy, endless ocean of wheat—brings nostalgia and retrospective angst as well. As the people begin to hibernate in their cozy homes because the chill is settling in, as the streets begin to empty out, and as I become slowly more aware of the isolation that surrounds, a specific kind of loneliness seeps into the bones, a loneliness that has also inspired books—that remote prairie desolation that either calls to the soul, or calls the spirit to lust for the twinkle of a city skyline at night, as it manifested for me.

The wild plains wind is a prairie queer prayer.

PRAYER 2: The prayer of the teenage weirdos in what felt like Nowhere, Saskatchewan, or some other small Canadian town. Canadian because of the yt rednecks who dominated there and who chased us into cities to begin with by repeating a cruelty, upheld for centuries, that they had inherited from their ancestors. The plains wind is a prayer for the prairie queers gazing out their bedroom windows, or the window of their parents' cars as they make their way to the next town over, into the emptiness of the vast sky, very sneakily, so secretly, dreaming about the debauchery that lies just beyond the horizon. A dream is just a wish the heart makes.[2]

This is for the slutty prairie queers who would stay up past midnight to watch Showcase after dark, with one hand on the remote in case they heard anyone upstairs stir—I feel you. The wayward, listless prairie youth who would watch *Party Monster*, before they knew how truly fucked up and cruel gay men could be, when gay communities still felt like enough to hold all the parts of them, if only for one night, dreaming of the day that they could glitter and shine their way to the middle. Out of the ass-kickings and slurs into the living, fucking, and loving. *'Cause on the surface the city lights shine. They're calling at me, "Come and find your kind."*[3]

Me, an Indigenous/gender studies scholar: Don't gender and sexualize nature. The wind is a relation whose gender is fluid and unknown to us, and it still affects everyone and everything it touches. Also me: The prairie wind is gay af. The prairie wind propels the queer body forward in a way shared among queer kin who perpetually followed those sparkling lights on the landscape: that queer lust for the city, that home in the horizon, and that desire for queer possibility. *Don't dream it, be it*[4]; *measure your life in love*[5]; etc.

The prairie wind is a prairie queer prayer. Propelling me forward, it calls my queerest, wandering spirit beyond the horizon's end. It touches everyone. It loves everyone. It exhilarates—gets everyone high. It's a club kid, really, and it just wants everyone to think it looks *real cute* and for all the prairie queers to follow it to the next great spot that only they know because their best friend nrg knows the promoter and can get us in for free. No sleeping, bitch, the prairie wind says, just pop an upper and let's catch the next train.

Queerness

I'm not talking about identity. I'm talking about bodies.
—*Caleb Luna*

When Indigenous people ask me the question, But why do you have to be queer? Why can't you just be Indian? I know they're actually questioning why I need to be so yt, and probably why I have to be such a dyke, too. The question about my need to be "queer" comes with underlying implications of shame and homophobia, and a little gaslighting on the back end, too—the suggestion that I'm not Indian enough because I have to appeal to colonial gender and sexuality to speak truth to fire.

Let's reframe the question in reverse. Instead of Indigenous folks asking me why I have to be queer, they could ask the Elder who refused to hug me in ceremony because I told them I was 2s why they did that. NDNs who want to ask me the question could instead ask the chief of the community where we gathered for water ceremony why he wouldn't let us have a 2s sweat. Not in his lodge, he said, even though he had taken a group of settlers there just the day before. Or maybe NDNs who ask the question just want to remind me what an asshole I am for marrying a yt boi, that I'm responsible for the loss of our bloodlines, and/or how colonized I am for getting married in the first place. NDN folks who want to inquire about my queer failure, my coinciding ytness, will question me in the same ways I've been questioned thousands of times before, like Native men haven't been leaving their mark on my body since before nikâwiy and Creator even gave it to me, and like social services didn't destroy my family. I'll sign any colonial paper that might afford me the smallest chance to keep my family together, now. How about we just call it even and chalk it up to a crisis in masculinities? See also: capitalism, colonialism.

After all these years, I still don't know how to talk about homophobia and transphobia on the rez. I'm not supposed to say the truth and give in to settler desire to consume my trauma and feed yt saviour ego, so at some dinner party settlers can use my book to talk about how they read a gay NDN's memoir and it said that it's *so violent* on the rez for gay NDNs—but, like, it's *so violent* on the rez for gay NDNs! I don't know how to deal with the tension between respecting my Elders and not accepting homophobic behaviour. I'm especially unsure how to admit that I so strongly identify with queerness, at least partially, because there was no place in Indigenous community for me to embody the love that was blooming inside of me. *I want to do everything. What a beautiful feeling.*[1]

When my Saulteaux, Cree, and Métis kin met in the Red River, they knew things were dire. They came together and created singular camps with—and shared identities out of—the desire for mutual survivance. Decades later in my own migrations to the seedy underbellies of the cities I ran to, I would find queer kinship. This is why "the question" seems so superficial—one-sided—to me. NDNs who ask the questions are asking, Why don't you claim me?

How can you betray our shared survival? As if they ever claimed me to begin with.

My queer and trans kinship networks are constellations of support made in the cities I ran to, away from cis- and hetero-normative violence and relations. After all, it was urban youth who raised me, who gave me their last pack of instant noodles, a spot in their single bed, and sips off their Old Style Pilsner when I was running. Queer is the family I have built in these places I've called home; made on endless stretches of highway roads, sweaty dance floors, and a cheeky substance-fuelled kiss or two. At BBQs, at rallies, around kitchen tables, at meetings, and in gutters, we created our families into being out of nothing. Us queers brought with us to the city our broken bones, our tired blood, our own secret traumas, and we were met with love. Queer love. Is there anything more pure? No, not in terms of its political power as a subversive counterculture. Rather, queer love is revolutionary love. Queer love revolutionizes love. You may call me romantic, or argue the trauma bond is corrupt, but at the core of it all, isn't love just the act of being seen, heard, and understood?[2] All of my queer and trans NDN friends are traumatized. Aren't we worthy of love, of kinships bonds, regardless of the quality of care we can give or receive?

I once read through my collection of old journals hoping to unearth writing about my body that I imagined was inevitably there. I used to obsess about my body. I painted the proportions of my body on the walls of my bedroom: grotesque and obscure rolls of flesh that were so distorted they almost seemed surreal, as if it didn't make sense, even in my own mind. Years later in therapy I would talk circles around the problem of dysphoria or fat shame? ADD or dissociation? Are these things even separate?

I disgusted myself and felt an insistent and inconsolable grief about the way my body was in this world. Because everywhere I looked in that small prairie town I grew up in were the perfect pure princesses of the empire with their tidy waists, whose stomachs didn't protrude over their pants, whose thighs didn't rub raw and red in the summertime, and whose breasts almost seemed to float, levitate, up and away from their bodies, while mine had sagged and drooped since the fourth grade. Yet somehow, the entries about my body that I had anticipated weren't there.

When I do eventually write about my body, at least that I can find within my journals, it's in March 2006 when I was nineteen years old.

> VISION 3: It is 12 a.m. before the drugs kick in, we make a fashionably late entrance, and it is hard finding a pickup. We get two whites for thirty, a decent price for the party we are at. All bad lighting and bad remixes. The high comes from the ground and enters slowly upward, like a heat rising. Recognizing the blitz, I immediately situate myself on the dance floor to let the music speak. I recognize the usual rush of an E high: the temperature change, the focus on texture and feel. And all at once, I come to life.

So it was that MDMA, and queer love, forced me into my body: my mouth against another mouth, and my sweaty skin pressed against the rest of the crowd. And it was the dance floor that facilitated queer love. Every weekend, without fail, my young queer kin and I would situate ourselves on dance floors of the prairie rave scene, in an abandoned warehouse or a rented community centre, chasing feeling. We had all been dissociated from our bodies too long, told they were sick with fem mannerisms and thick thighs that were just a little too plentiful, too greedy, for public space. As queer kin, we gifted each other the ability to name desires I had been told I wasn't worthy of, and let me believe I'm worthy of love, worthy to take up space, and worthy of being fucked, in the small-town queer communities we birthed at those seedy warehouse raves. *Standing in the way of control, you live your life, survive the only way that you know.*[3]

Was it Hollinghurst who said the gay novel is dead, even though he should have just said that the yt dude gay novel is dead? The gay bar was still a spark, a generative force for me, a space wherein my queer ethics, family, and body came to life. And me and my kin are only just gaining the space to talk about how queer dance floors regenerate our colonized bodies, since that LGBTQ+ thing has been more like a yt LG thing for a long minute. The only difference is that now I'm able recognize the gay bar as an unending reminder of my undesirability and disappearance, and my status as a full-fledged colonial object—the living dead in ghost worlds.[4]

VISION 4: wâkâyôs

I drive through the streets of downtown Regina in a car with my high school friends, probably best described as yt punks. As we drive down Scarth, we pass our local haunt: a bar called O'Hanlon's. Outside stands my brother wâkâyôs. Our glances catch each other as my friends and I drive by in our car. I see a smirk on wâkâyôs's face that I recognize so clearly, a look that can only be described by something he said to me once: "You're the ytest Indian I know."

Maybe so. Maybe when I cut off my hair, bleached the brown out of what was left, and dyed it blue. When I ornamented my skin, pierced it, branded it, and modified it so it was less *ethnic, ancient*; more *modern, yt*. Like my yt friends shielding me from the settler gaze, or the Indian question,[1] as they say. I wanted to be absorbed into the body politic—hide in plain view.

Creation Story

I gave birth to a universe at nineteen years old. I got on a Greyhound bus with my lover, who I will call Back to Black (B2B), a name I gave them to describe a love so intense—full of addiction, mistrust, lies, and abuse that we reasoned away as passion—that it could only be compared to Amy Winehouse's album of the same name. We headed toward the closest big city: Edmonton (Deadmonton or Oil-town). That's how the common-folk got around the prairies—by hurtling down its endless highways in a beat-up old Greyhound. The lack of air conditioning and locked anti-suicide windows made the ride so hot that passengers' thighs stuck to the gaudily upholstered seats, which hadn't been updated since the 1980s, and were stiff and scratchy like a towel with dried semen on it. There was always that middle-aged biker, sans bike, with his leather vest and Harley Davidson tattoos, offering his seatmate swigs off a forty half-assedly concealed in a paper bag. I remember the horizon seeming just a little out of reach, no matter how many hours we passed driving those dusty prairie roads, and the journey endless like maybe I'd continually be on the move. *If the world's at large, why should I remain?*[1]

The living skies made the terrain look infinite, like a never-ending sea of gold and green. The land was speckled with a broken-down farm here, and a decaying wheat elevator there—all remnants of western settlement come to pass before everyone moved to the city, and the disappearance of my Cree, Métis, and Saulteaux ancestors. The Depression era destroyed the small-farm economy of my yt settler relatives and imprisoned my Cree, Métis, and Saulteaux ones within extreme poverty and/or the reserve system—an economic shift that destroyed the prosperity of rural Saskatchewan communities, and the blame for which yt rural communities transferred onto racialized migrant communities and Indigenous Peoples.

My mom and dad were there to see me off on my first big move out of the prairie town where I grew up. My mom seemed small sitting in her wheelchair. I had no idea how sick she was. Our relationship was never secure, but she always wanted to do the right thing, like see me off that day. My mom would die only ten years later, when I was leaving on my final (and farthest) run away yet, after having run from their home multiple times since the age of fourteen. For once, she couldn't stop me. I was an adult now.

I used to have nightmares about causing my mom's death.

VISION 5: I dream that I am studying for a stats exam the next day and my mom has a heart attack. I call 911 and keep trying to get ahold of my dad who is unreachable. I panic, frantically trying to reach someone to come save her, but for some reason I keep failing to get through to anyone, which only makes me more frustrated and irate—a familiar trigger response to anxiety and fear—my hands shaking so I can no longer dial the

phone. A nurse in a cab comes to help, but neither of us knows how to use the defibrillators. My
mom dies in front of me. I remember the underlying feeling of the dream being that I am responsible, that I have killed her.

My mom and I hadn't been speaking before her death, and
only reconnected shortly beforehand. What started as a
casual phone call from her following a major breakup, because she was worried about me, became semi-regular
phone calls that were light-hearted and cautious, some of
our first contact in over three years. Even then, we were
just easing ourselves back into what both of us had known
to be shark-infested waters. My mom and I had fallen out
of contact after an intense fight. I have no idea what started it, or what the final blow was that created the silence
and distance between us. That's how innocuous it was,
and how intense the tension between us had become, that
it took one fight to sever our relationship so severely and
for so long.

Telling the story of me and my mom feels like an attempt to reconcile the irreconcilable, mainly because I've
lost her side of this story, and can only weave together our
history from my memories. Still, I've had The Truth of yt
men supersede my own for so long that there is something
empowering about at least trying to piece together my side
of our relationship. But I still struggle to ethically unravel
the intricacies of her emotional abuse, the kind that lasts
decades, slowly chipping away at the spirit, and likely de-
rived from her fear, loneliness, and loss of independence
from illness. My mom feared loss of control, having always
been the master of her own life, so she sought to control
me. A friend once described chronic, incapacitating illness

to me as waking up in the midst of a panic attack, feeling claustrophobic and trapped in your body. Making me think of my mom, their description touched me. She was lonely, alone in her house all day, while the rest of us continued to live our lives, and she was cut off from the community she had loved so dearly—she and the pills. It was an ironic cycle though, because as she turned more to the pills for comfort, she became more incapacitated, more of an invalid, as my dad once put it.

I don't know what else to do now other than forgive and hope she forgave me—and even then it would just be for me, to reconcile my own unrest. I know that she never meant to project all her quickly dying hopes and desires onto me, viewing my body as an extension of her own moral imperative toward conformity through the creation of the perfect home. I understand drug addiction as a way of coping with the loss of control over one's life—a hell of a thing. I don't blame her, any more than I blame nikâwiy for having nothing left to give me. You could say a lot of things about my mom and nikâwiy, and the choices they made, to let me go, to attain me, but they did what they could for me and did what they could to survive. Honouring the efforts my women kin put into who I am today, I own the scars their negotiations left on my body.

I mourned my mom before we burned her body because we had created a silence between us so deafening I had already felt years of grief about her loss. I had spent so much of my teenage and adult life running from her grasp because it felt suffocating, just as her illness was suffocating to her. Cyclical smothering.

I want to be careful when dredging up the past because memories confound. I have to deal with a black hole of unresolved feelings now, but still, there is no regret. At the time, I had to choose myself. I put fifty-two city blocks between my parents and myself and, when that proved to be not enough, finally a province. Neither of us knew then how little time we had left, that day when she saw me off. All that wasted time would pass so quickly for me. Silent days would turn into silent months, sometimes, and into the final silence before her death. Eventually I would put five more provinces between us, and then an ocean. But I didn't know it that day, at the Greyhound station. That day she was just beaming with pride and love from her wheelchair, trying to support me.

My friend Walker was at the Greyhound station the day I left, too. He started to tear up as I got on the bus. I felt so awkward that I half-snorted, half-laughed. Ours was a sacred covenant of two queer teenagers, that first intense friend love, where it's you against the whole sick, sad world[2] and you binge on spending time with one another, trying to devour every bit of one another, greedy for the satisfaction of being understood, appreciated, and accepted, as you are. Our friend group had coordinated our outfits for our senior photos, so we were all wearing button-up T-shirts under dark-coloured sweaters and thick-framed plastic glasses, while donning a scowl instead of the typical school photo smile, a reaction to one of our classmates calling us "the emo crew." When we got the proofs we all signed the back of the mock-up photos and gave them to one another, all of our 'I's dotted with tiny 'X's, assuring one another that we would love each other for always. But the truth is that you become so many people after that period, you're lucky if you can endure all that transformation and still feign relating to the people you brought close during the emotional upheaval that is high school. I've advised people close to me that one shouldn't get too caught up in a single person, place, group of people, and accidently hold oneself back. The wind should always be followed onto the next town, the next opportunity, and all the possible loves that are waiting out there. But, that's coming from a self-proclaimed runner.

Walker and I shared that exhilaration of the premier weirdo-4-weirdos vibe; of staying out until dawn, driving out of the city limits, parking our car, and sitting on the hood to watch the sunrise while some embarrassing emo band was playing out of the speakers. *Would you die tonight for love?*[3] I, too, felt sadness and mourning for breaking that sacred bond, and leaving him to face the harsh prairie terrain alone. But we still had plenty of other weirdos to have intense friendships with, in the cities where we respectively ran, and we didn't know yet how different a yt gay male and an NDN queer were, in the grand scheme of that LGBTQ2+ umbrella.

Though there were some glimmers of hope in Regina, I hated it and everything I had endured there. I hated the rednecks who called me a fat Indian bitch at school, but came a-knocking (as Grandma Edna might say) on the weekends, all wanting a taste of that sweet caramel they heard was so easily conquered. Fuck teachers (all yt men, of course) who told me I wouldn't graduate from high school, that I'd never amount to anything, and that I didn't belong in advanced classes. I left behind all the kids who couldn't play with me because they weren't "allowed to play with Indians." Funny, it was always the adults who were the most racist and antagonizing figures in my life, not the kids. That same mother called my school's principal to narc on me, telling them that I was a "witch" to protect her perfect yt children from my brown devilish ways. I once heard someone say that calling the cops on a Black person is attempted murder. What is it called when security culture and disposable Native bodies meet in the form of an uppity suburban yt lady? *The Craft* had just come out and my friends and I went through a goth phase, like every yt girl at my elementary school. But no one else had their "phase" taken as a serious threat, and their teacher pull them aside to tell them they were in trouble.

Driving out of the city, one of the last things I saw was the Sears warehouse. Just off the Ring Road and built in the 1970s, it was a giant industrial building that had at one time housed Sears operations, an archive of the brutalist architecture throughout Regina. Unpretentious and unassuming, its contents a little bit cheaper than you'd find in the big city, it was the perfect metaphor for Regina. You had to drive past it leaving and entering the city from the north, and at night it would light up. Day or night, it always seemed lonely, sitting by itself in an empty field, badly deteriorating before its demolition in 2016. It was like the Hollywood sign, but much less impressive. But before its destruction, no matter where I was or where I'd been, the Sears sign was always there to let me back in.

Before Edmonton had come penance. I did a stint at an oil camp cleaning rooms and serving food to riggers, about an hour north of Fort McMurray. Their rooms were always filthy. Everything was coated in black dirt, and the bathrooms reeked of urine only a day after being cleaned. I saw more porn than I'd ever seen in my life. Stacked high on the nightstands were magazines, erotica, skin-flicks, or manga—take your pick. Porn taped up on the wall staring at you while you cleaned. Of course, there was always the guy with the fetish, and I'd find a collage of vaguely racialized women staring back at me from a headboard. The

racialized women appeared more sexualized than yt wom-
en in nudie magazines: bent over with their ass in your
face, cheeks spread, and all low-quality lighting and disco-
louration. These workers saw that when they looked at me.

The camp consisted of a series of isolated portables
in the middle of a field, surrounded by a remaining portion of the forest likely left there to conceal the environ-
mental atrocities beyond. You saw the devastation when
you drove through the oil fields to get to camp, though. It
was akin to Mordor. The once beautiful rocky terrain was
clear-cut and there were no trees left visible on the sparse
terrain. The ground was all dug up, and all that remained
was the brown underearth, now exposed. Steel structures
were erected from the now barren territories, some with
fire roaring from their tops that billowed smoke into the
sky, a never-ceasing reminder of the oil industry's rule in
Alberta. The land was sick and I knew I was reaping the
benefits of its sickness. But I was only nineteen and poor
as hell. I had no work experience, and even less big city
experience, and you could make a hefty stack in just three
weeks of overtime in camp. That Red River blood running
through my veins, that ingenuity and that lust for the fur
trade, equally problematic. I was following the river networks of my ancestors across the prairies in search of
some money to put food on the table and to fund my ad-
venture, survivance, and hopefully, queer love.

One morning when I left my dorm and started walking toward the common room, my eyes went blurry and
the hall stretched out in front of me. I continued walking, focussing on the door at the end of the hallway, but
no matter how far I had progressed, it never seemed to
get closer. I knew I was starting to crack, like I had seen
nikâwiy do many times before—one of my guiltiest and

most pervasive fears. I was making fifty-five beds seven days a week and using carcinogenic chemicals, which made my chest hurt, in enclosed spaces. I would spend my days dreaming and gazing out the windows at the trees outside, listening to Pavement on my iPod. We were engulfed by the boreal forest, parasites to that land, polluting the woods and all its inhabitants. Somehow I was frequently overwhelmed by the freshness of the forest that remained, the spruce collectively exhaling oxygen for all their relations, the forest's perseverance.

> PRAYER 3: Thank you to all the trees who breathe in poison on the daily, who gift us the air that we breathe and the wind that propels everything forward.

And then, my birth. We were finally free from camp and pounding the pavement in Edmonton. Displaced, but still in my territories. It's that Cree-Métis-Saulteaux, city NDN thing, okay?

> VISION 6 is an MDMA high, the queerest of all visions. Everything is soft—focus, touch, your heart—and there's a tender, bright haze to the world. It's rose-tinted glasses, in pill form. It's serotonin pumping through you, and your body, mind, and feelings open and ready for the world. It's queer wonder's perfect companion. It's Saturday night. I can feel the blood pumping through my veins as the heat rises from the sidewalks and ushers me along on my misadventures. I'm a little faded on this and that. I'm wide-eyed at the dizzying effect of seeing all the lights

through my small-town eyes. The city twinkles in front of me unlike the dull glow of my hometown's streetlamps. The city centre is flashing and sparkly. As I drive into downtown via Saskatchewan Drive, Edmonton looks like the lights of thousands of tiny stars in the sky at midnight. The twilight of the city is glaring, blinding my Md-glazed eyes.

B2B and I made our way to the Roost, the oldest gay bar in western KKKanada before it closed to make way for condos and government buildings. The rest of downtown would follow. Social housing and the casino would eventually become Rogers Place, pushing out all the low-income people who used to inhabit Edmonton's downtown northeast neighbourhoods. B2B and I were trying to date other people while still living together in a bachelor apartment, during one of our brief stretches after breaking up wherein we would proceed to get back together in the following weeks. We were messy like that.

It was two floors of debauchery. *Blaze a blaze, purple haze—galang a lang a lang lang.*⁴ Upstairs was for the tweakers and the cruisers, a place I admit I found myself one night or two. They played music that people would probably call "dad house" now. The bottom floor played top forty and was where the dykes hung out. You'd also find the girls making conversation in the smoking pit out back, usually needing a little more chit-chat to pick up, whereas the guys had it down to a single look.

The smoking pit at the Roost is where I first saw nisîmis. Though I didn't know it then, she would be my longest love. She was wearing a Bikini Kill T-shirt featuring the record player from the cover of their singles album, for which I had a matching tattoo. In contemporary

Montreal this might be commonplace. But this was 2006 in Edmonton, when everyone wore designer brands, was or wanted a butch-fem, and had $150 Tegan and Sara haircuts. nisîmis had thick purple frames—a component of what she called her lesbrarian style—that were a blend of vintage irony and Le Tigre-esque radical lesbian feminism. She was wearing multiple cheesy plastic rosaries.

I had drunk enough that night to have the liquid courage to approach her and ask her about her T-shirt, under the guise of asking her for a light. She was smoking clove cigarettes and it created a fragrant haze around her. When she cracked a smile, her face was overwhelmed by her cheeks, her crooked little teeth were unabashedly exposed, and a smiley piercing hung down from her top lip. I couldn't take my eyes off her. I had never seen anyone like her before. It was the closest I've come to love at first sight. I created a mythos about her instantaneously that would remain for years and, of course, that she could never live up to. I could instantly see our deep lez life. We'd live in the serenity of some old apartment surrounded by all of her thrifted kitsch, me writing the novel I always talked about and her sewing, doors open to let in the summer afternoon in and the Nina Simone record we were playing into the street, where it belonged.

We walked home together and talked about how wearing makeup didn't mean we weren't feminists—fem power before it was cool. There was, and still is, a high premium on yt masculinities. Once back at her place, we passed out before either of us could make a move. But our love would be one for the ages.

It's pretty surreal to think about how far I've come and all the love I've been gifted. Thank Creator for that.

The Spatiality of Yt Gays[1]

First of all, you need to know that I am not the one.
—Rihanna

I've been dating yt queer alt kidz my whole life, who shamed me for listening to RnB because it was capitalist and objectified women. They did so not realizing that the journey to success for Bey, Nicki, and Riri had more punk rock spirit than they have in a single muscle of their trust-fund bodies, gentrifying the neighbourhoods traditionally occupied by people of colour in the cities where I've lived because of their desire to live like common people do.

Get your eyes off that difference, the yt gays say, just like they told me to keep my eyes off that money with their trust funds behind them. Just like an anarchist to blindly shove a political puritan envisioning of collective futures down my throat that erases class, gender, and ability. That's not the rev; that's just settler-colonial dystopic now, in a different flavour. Maybe anarchists / Marxists / rad queers should liquidate their trust funds and give them to the poor. That'd be super anarchy. Divest from their parents' rent payments. Resist the occupation of Berlin and Parc Ex. Nah, didn't think so. But, you know, ~liberalism~ or whatever.

There's always that yt that wants to say I'm "just

starting shit." Little grrrl, I think what you meant to say was that it makes you uncomfortable that I *don't take shit* and that I'm not quiet about it, when you've spent your whole life quieting yourself for the status quo, and now do the same in your supposedly radical queer community— supposedly because it's so easily shaken to the core by any request for emotional clarity and closure.

But that's the problem with queer spaces. Queer rad politics can succumb to their broad strokes, become wishful thinking with no political strategy or real-time rollout. It's that little grrrl's general statements about the politics of fucking and workers rising, which she read about in her international development (see also: colonialism) major, women's studies minor track at the uni they call the ivy of the north. It's why little grrrl fits so neatly at the throne of labour organizing, with its broad class application and none of that pesky intersectionality. #WhiteFeminism

Because little grrrl doesn't want to take the time to read any NDN or Black theory—"do you even read Black women?"[2]— to think through the specificity of experiences her rad crew purports to make space for. And all this while her best grrrlfriend is out here getting into physical fights at queer raves because she can't handle herself when she gets too high. Performative politics are the ones we don't live.

What constitutes a community? Because it surely isn't the same yt bois who have tantrums at HIV organizing meetings when it's mentioned that the AIDS crisis in KKKanada is an Indigenous one, or who let some yt Quebecois fuckhead call my friend a racial slur intended for Black folks at the prison justice event where they showed the same basic, yt gay art film noir they'd shown a thousand times before.

Stop trying to hold me accountable to communities I never consented to be a part of, little grrrl. I know who my queer community is—who feels me, who sees me—and, yes, that has included many a politicized yt. But that ain't you, little grrrl. What makes you think that Creator put me here to put up with your shit? Who's got time for taking shit when the world is ending and I've got 2s kin to look out for? Like, real deal street kids, y'know? Except we don't glamourize street life, because we've actually lived the street life and it isn't romantic in the slightest. The streets are where you self-make,[3] and where yt men make me disappear.

I'm not your fat NDN friend, or your fat NDN fuck, who fills out an identity quota for you—okay? Gay is not the new Black, as nisîmis would say. Don't forget, I'm that gen that saw the shift from cisgender lesbian/gay centricity to complex gender analysis. I still remember when yt gays told me that genderqueer is just "hipster for lesbian." And, like, why do yt gays dress like squeegee kids, like poverty is an aesthetic, even though they've never had to worry about rent or food a single day of their lives? Even worse, they mark their bodies as if to racialize them—pierce them the same ways we did (do), tattoo them with tribal designs, and dye their hair away from its ashy blonde colour. I've shared many a dance floor with yt dreads, mohawks, and even a dread-hawk or two. *Très poseur*, tbh. You wouldn't know counterculture if you saw it. Being brown and/or Black has never been in style. Yt queers visibly mark their body so they can know difference. But they can just as easily access the signifiers of wealth and ytness again and integrate back into ~respectable~ society if they want to.

When yt gays take up a little (a lot) too much space in

community meetings, I see them. When a yt gay reacts with fragility when a BIPOC organizer points out toxic yt-ness in community organizing space, I see them. When a yt gay soapboxes in a meeting "just to ask a question," I see them. When a yt gay tries to micromanage me though we supposedly work in non-hierarchal and consensus-based environments, I see them. When a yt gay tells me that I am "being aggressive" when I react to presumption, entitlement, and unspoken power—their spatiality—I see them.

Still, it's forty years after *This Bridge Called My Back*, wherein Chrystos famously declared, *We are both in danger of your ancient fear.* It was the yt gays who enacted the silencing logics of queer love to tell us, We are all the same in the fight against the heteros. No, we can't talk about colonialism in this meeting. We're talking about class, not race. The agenda is already too packed for more identity politics. Of course I know what racism feels like, I've been called the f-word.

In yt gays, I see the fair-skinned princes(ses) of a colonial empire whose right to this land has been told to them again and again, who quenched their milky skin in bathfuls of my ancestors' blood, and who were taught from a young age that, no matter how mediocre, they deserve a place in this world and they need only reach out and grab it, even if that place is performative poverty and downward class mobility. Sharing a beer with me at the local gay haunt does not absolve yt queers of the histories of dominance associated with their being in the world, on this land.

Yt gays act like writers and organizers who centre race and Indigeneity are so sensitive but, like, hell hath no fury like a yt gay told (s)he is, indeed, yt, or, heavens forbid, met with a boundary.

The yt queers say, We all belong here—here being in the queer community, whatever that is, here on the dance floor, or here in this dive bar trying to find the truth in one another's bodies and a little powder of choice up the nose (or down the hatch).

Before you go all yt family values on me, know that we chase the feeling now because we've had that feeling beaten, tortured, and shamed out of us for millennia. We live loud and glittery for all our queer ancestors who couldn't, who lived in hiding or who lost their lives for chasing the feeling; and also for the ones who stick it to the man by loving and fucking, regardless, so that we may now repeat. We scream into the night for our bohemian forefathers, doing queer ceremony in their names, except the absinthe has been replaced with Molly, and truth, love, and beauty[4] are dancing with soft butch bois to a grimy Missy song. I remember that heady rush of walking into a gay bar for the first time. The catty quick wit of a yt boi who had grown up in a prairie town that wanted to destroy him—who was still slaying, despite it all, because of it all. Yt gays were some of my first queer kin. I want to be clear, my dearest queers, queer is my home, too. I believe in kinship and, dejected, I have found queer kin on a dance floor or two.

But yt queers claim "here" so effortlessly because it's their space. They don't see, or maybe don't want to admit, the ways that queer visualities and signifiers are made to fit their bodies. "Here," where skinny yt masc is always on trend, and we flag using visual markers that reify colonial gender binaries on Indigenous bodies through fem/masc binaries—like whether or not you have long hair and wear lipstick. You've made a lovely home—haven't you—"here," on my flesh and of my bones?

My Native friends tell me I dress like a hipster. I guess I've just been queer flagging for so long, trying to be seen and not seen all at once, that now I have a permanent attraction to a good pair of frames.

Queen City Punk

There's a nostalgia about queer community. Most of us were getting beaten up in high school, so now we relive youthful moments—puberty, prom, crushing. Queer alt and punk scenes are similar: they recreate spaces queers were pushed out of in their teens, for us to relive and become twisted icons within. But perhaps I never felt a romantic draw to the queer punk scenes in the cities I ran to because I had already survived a queer punk scene in my hometown during my youth. Sometimes it feels like we're all just perpetually surviving various scenes, in different times and places.

As a teen in the Queen City, before my friends and I had cars, we'd take the bus to the north end and go to tailgate parties with the other punk kids at the skate park, which at the time was the farthest I had ever strayed from home on my own. True teenage dirtbags,[1] countless afternoons and evenings we would smoke weed and listen to new CDs. Drunk on the youthful exhilaration of trying out our freedom, we'd pile into one of our friends' cars afterward, drive up and down Albert Street with the windows down, and scream our favourite punk and emo songs. Yeah, we were nihilists. Could you blame us? George W Bush was the president of the United States, we thought the world was going to blow up, and our parents wouldn't admit that America was the terrorist.[2]

My friends and I would plan for shows we wanted to go to on the weekend because there was always one on somewhere in our small-town music scene that started out as Queen City Punk and would later transform into Queen City Hardcore when the music, and the scene bros who played it, shifted. We would research local shows on the Queen City Punk ProBoard message board, where I was LINZ*OI. We'd also frequent message boards linked to the GeoCities websites of local bands, posting on several different message boards a day. That's what kept us moving forward: the anticipation of ramming our bodies into other youth at a punk show the following weekend.

On Friday or Saturday nights you could walk over the bridge at Saskatchewan and Albert, follow the train tracks up to the warehouse district, and catch a show at the Exchange. The Exchange was in an area that was sparsely populated, composed of mostly old factories and warehouses. It was eerily close to North Central and the Piapot urban rez—yt gentrification at its apex, which I didn't know about yet. You could also go downtown and cross Victoria Park to hit up the Buffalo Lounge, a part of the Baptist church where the pastor would let youth run punk shows. Sometimes we'd get lucky, and a touring band would come through Regina. We'd start amping one another up weeks in advance for when the Dropkick Murphys, The Distillers, or AFI were in town—our idols in simpler times, who we saw as Gods among men.

Some weekends we'd pile into an old beater and drive out to Swift Current, Saskatoon, Estevan, or Moose Jaw to catch a show at a legion or community centre. The small-town punk scenes of these little prairie towns existed in what felt like a frozen empty tundra, connecting us where it seemed connections weren't possible. We were that generation who went from analog to digital. We'd log onto our parents dial-up, and its insistent screech would be our soundtrack as we reached into the open web to make some of the first viral and internet-based music scenes. All you needed was to download some recording freeware, like FruityLoops, and a MySpace profile for your project. Or you could just go old school and record an EP, then burn it onto a blank CD from your parents' computer to hand out at shows. There was something about isolation and creation that just went together. Perhaps the best art happens when there's nothing to distract us, and we can only be in ourselves, with one another. The digital indie movement was just picking up so there were a few groups who sounded like The Postal Service. But mostly the scene was a cheap reproduction of hardcore groups like Throwdown and Hatebreed.

The punk youth I would go to shows with were the people I would run to when I was running from my parents. I'd squat with them in downtown Regina apartments where there was no furniture, and we all slept on the old hardwood floors. I'd go as a backup when they went to shady houses to party and smoke heroin for the first time. We were young, and it was a time when all we had was that punk youth, street fam, and our atheist belief that we could live forever tonight, in a world we were sure was going to end because of global warming and America's invasion of Iraq for resource extraction.

The other side of punk scenes that evolved with the help of the internet, a phenomenon that indeed trickled down into Queen City Punk, is the racists and the skinheads. When I see archival photos of QCP now, it's always the same sea of yt faces, conveniently glossing over the fact that Queen City Punk was largely made up of folks who were openly skinhead punks. Somehow the skinheads removed this aesthetic from racism, assuring critics that their looks were a countercultural reference and their choice of fashion had nothing to do with race. They were listening to Skrewdriver "just for the music." QCP was that message board bro rhetoric in real life. It came up on the ProBoards that we came up on. It's like calling someone the f-word, and having Pepe cartoons as your profile photo, and having other yt bros come to your defence because you're a "stand-up" guy. Trolls who are actually low-key yt supremacists, and high-key misogynists—that's what composed a lot of Queen City Punk.

The physical violence that put women at risk was another early awakening to the scene's inherent patriarchal masculinism. At a certain point, the music and bands started to change. People weren't listening to punk anymore. It was this new sound coming in—hardcore—that had breakdowns, donned vocals that sounded like hoarse shouting, and band logos in Old English or boarding school lettering. I'm told its roots are in rap, metal, and hardcore punk—all things heavy, you could say. Melody wasn't metal enough, I guess. *For my family forever,*[3] *if you don't live for something you'll die for nothing,*[4] etc. The pits were a little more violent when the scene started changing. I didn't always feel safe. Squabbles would break out between the punks who wanted to circle pit and the hardcore kids who had more elaborate dancing. The presence of skinheads in the punk scene is likely what led to the shift toward hardcore. But a class divide also emerged in the scene's shift in sound. Namely, the kids from the burbs were the ones who took on hardcore and popularized it in the Queen City, and the street kids, the squeegee kids, remained true to punk.

Then there are the rapists. I don't think I had a single friend at the time who hadn't hooked up with a guy twice her age who was out on tour, most of whom had a wife and kids back home. Suspicious stories seemed to follow them too, of girls blacking out when they partied with them, only to wake up the next morning in bed next to one of these guys. Except, it wasn't just predatory guys in touring bands. Older men from the Regina punk scene who we'd see every Friday night at the Exchange were constant MySpace lurkers.

It took me so long to understand that QCP was a yt man's world, just like everything else on the prairies. Eventually I heard about riot grrrl: about bashing back when you aren't safe in the pit, about cock-rock assholes, and about rape in the punk music scene.

When I attended one of my first underground raves, some of the hardcore kids were throwing a show in the next room and came over to make fun—just to laugh. I was tongue deep in my first fem's mouth and caught up in that intoxicating rush of early 2000s synth and ecstasy (before they were both too speedy) when I turned and caught their mocking gaze. Evoking my queer ancestors before me, I was too high to care.[5] There was no room for dykes in Queen City Hardcore, and I turned back to the truth, newly found rooted in her mouth.

By the time I graduated from the scene, I felt beaten down like there was no place for women and queers, and the only place for folks who weren't men was as "groupies" or superfans. I guess it's like my friend told me when we were smoking up in his car in the parking lot of Victoria Square mall: men just can't identify with the female voice. We were listening to Metric, and before he had said it, I had been spacing out on Emily's lyrics and intricate guitar-pop melodies, imagining a world beyond this shitty east end, teenage love song. *Fight off the lethargy. Don't go quietly. Combat baby. Said you would never give up easy.*[6]

Despite everything, I still loved the scene and its music. I was still piling into cars full of grrrls, and driving up to Estevan to catch Propagandhi and Tsunami Bomb, leaving the show drenched in sweat from the pit and with a voice hoarse from scream-singing all night. It might make me sound like a mosh pit bro, but moshing felt so feminist to my friends and me because we had never been allowed to move our bodies in those ways before. I still have a bad ankle from Regina's mosh pits. I have scars on my body from QCP.

Death Machine

I've known that poverty lives on the body for a minute but I guess the daughters call that body horror now.

The hardest drugs to do are the ones you have to snort. It's all about mustering the courage to deal with the burn. I just snorted two lines of Dexedrine. My teeth are already chattering. I got it from my downstairs neighbour. She's on welfare but, of course, they never give her enough, so she has to sell her prescription.

I'm supposed to be cleaning my shithole apartment and doing something productive. Instead, I'm thinking about the first time I bled, and how memories are tricky. Memories are a dream that we piece together in the aftermath of happenings and events.

I remember asking my mom about my first period in an email, asking her what she could recall from that moment. Her response surprised me because my memory was so different.

I have many fond memories of you growing up. I remember you calling me at work to let me know you had started your period. I had tried to give you the information you would need to prepare you for the upcoming event. No matter how prepared you think you are it is a big and scary event. I was working

days (12 hours) and was disappointed that I wasn't
home for you. I managed to find someone to work
the last four hours for me.

The way I remember it, I was in our upstairs bathroom
when I realized I was bleeding. My mom reluctantly came
up after I called out to her several times. She had been
waiting in the front foyer with my dad because we were
about to go out for dinner. Years later I would reread *Are
You There God? It's Me, Margaret* for a university course
about girlhoods, and I would find out that Margaret's first
period experience was closely aligned with my own. Had
I made up the memory, adopted it from this book I had
read so many times as a pre-teen? But my mom's recol-
lection of my first bleed was also remarkably similar to
the one she told me about hers. She said my grandma was
working, and she had to use tea towels my great-grandmother provided for her to absorb the blood, just as she
had done throughout her Depression era youth. Whose
version of the story about my first bleed is right, mine or
my mother's, will never be reconciled. I'm the only one
left to carry our story forward—which is perhaps why I
cautiously wade through remembering with a hint of cynicism. Because whose truth is The Truth, you know? And I
need to be accountable to the fact that I still effect, and affect, firmly rooted in worlds I have constructed for myself
in memories (dreams), regardless of if the other memory
participants can give their side of my truth.

When I try to piece together the happenings surround-
ing my miscarriage, at least the ones I didn't repress, the
most pronounced sense memory is from the downtown
Regina public library, one of the only free things to do in
the area. I would cruise the stacks for hours, thumbing

through *Dykes to Watch Out For*, checking MySpace on the internet terminals that would time out after an hour, reading the latest issue of *Bitch* magazine, and perusing the CDs for new bands to download on LimeWire. I was on the internet terminals when the blood gushed down my legs.

I also remember bleeding, shitting without control, and puking all over the bathroom floor. I was back at my parent's house having left the hospital after admitting myself because of the bleed out at the library—alone, passing out, and rolling around in the fluids my body rejected. In so much pain I couldn't even sit up, let alone call for help. The doctor refused to give me a D&C at the hospital, instead deciding to send me home with the abortion pill against my request and without a blood cell count. Luckily I lost so much blood that I passed out before I could take the second dose. Lucky because I could have died. Unlucky because the yt doctor didn't care if I died because he saw another pregnant Indian he didn't want to treat. Maybe next time I'd use a condom, he probably thought.

A week later, I was back in the hospital with a uterus infection that could have made me sterile, a blood cell count that was nearly fatal, and in need of two blood transfusions.

They said, You're a sorry excuse for a lesbian. Wasn't he supposedly "gay" too? If your girlfriend has a penis, she isn't a girlfriend. You were going to have an abortion anyhow.

But no one saw the blood, felt the pain, and felt it pass. No one else almost died or almost went sterile. No one except me, with my partner at the time, Kai. Kai was my queer, baby trans-feminine lover. When I met her, she quickly became my gay best friend. As her gender evolved, as we evolved through the rush of the Queen City industrial rave scene, we fell in love. We conceived. We became bad lesbians.

The hardest drugs to do are the ones you snort. Well, those, and the ones prescribed by straight yt male doctors who want to feed you to the death machine when you're only nineteen years old. I just snorted two Dexedrine, and I think I'll sit around in my own filth today, just like yesterday, and the day before, and the day before. Maybe today will be the day my roof is torn off by the prairie wind, exposing me to the open sky. I'll close my eyes and soar into the emptiness.

Concrete Warriors

I'd been running away from home since I was fourteen, bolting into the night as quick as my legs would carry me, leaving behind, well, whatever event I was running from—which I won't list here. Consider this a reminder, dear reader: thank you for reading but, while I feel no pressure to hide my pain from you and ground my story in neoliberalism, I don't owe you my pain.

My apartment on 14th Avenue and Hamilton Street was the first place that was ever just mine. Humble as it may have been, this tiny bachelor apartment, with an even smaller bathroom, was the first place that ever belonged to me alone. Not a squat of teen punks, not a lover's bed, a friend's floor after sneaking in their window once their parents were asleep, or a hostel bunk—when my body was the only place I had to call home, and even then it still felt like rented space some days.

PRAYER 4 is a riff-raff, city NDN prayer. Cree-Métis-Saulteaux sovereignty isn't about nationhood, some invisible prison that contains our identities within colonial parameters. Cree-Métis-Saulteaux sovereignty is where Cree-Métis-Saulteaux peoples stand. It's a people (peoples). When you lose place, because your ancestors did what they needed to do so you'd

survive, your body, your community, becomes your
home and sovereignty.

Wholly and entirely alone, I jumped on my single prin-
cess bed with hearts along the frame, full of novelty and
exhilaration from this newfound independence. I listened
to Magneta Lane, danced around my kitchen, and felt the
emptiness and isolation, in the seclusion of that prairie
town. I was also alone with my own head, with my emptiness, trying to chase away that inherited crazy I could feel
percolating below the surface, increasingly clouding my
mind ever since puberty. I typically didn't have enough
money to pay my bills, let alone buy a computer. All I had
was one of the early Nokia phones. Even though I only
had five or six analog tapes, I would play them on repeat
on an old hand-me-down TV with dials on the front. I'd always have something playing in the background, even if it
was just white noise. Baz Luhrmann's *Romeo + Juliet* was
a favourite. Once a self-hating English major, I had a soft
spot for Luhrmann's gay Black Mercutio.

I don't know how to describe Hamilton Street other than it was grimy. I don't mean grimy in a demeaning
way. There was just a city grit to that period of my life. I
was poor and thinner than I had ever been because I was
barely eating. Sometimes I'd have $30 to eat for two weeks,
so I'd exclusively eat PB&J sandwiches and buttered noodles for days straight. I only lived four blocks away from
O'Hanlon's, which was the bar that I went to on Saturday
nights when it was always packed to the walls because
they played Justice and MGMT. The Organ played there
once, and none of the scene showed up except budding alt
girls in their late teens and early twenties, grateful to finally see some music we identified with and a band whose

drummer we could crush on. Most of my extra money went into many a pint on the O'Hanlon's patio and dance floor.

Some nights I would hang out with a gay boi who lived across the hall. We'd take pills and go to raves, which is where I directed the rest of my income. I was utterly obsessed with the rush of queer nightlife. Loving, fucking, and feeling ourselves back to life every night among the small town party full of fairies, butches, and neo–club kids. You'd see the same people every Friday night, all of our eyes a little glazed, fixed on something just a little more than this. Queer kin were some of my first kin. We were there to sneer at the cops who picked up Cedar and Lake on the faerie strip across from our apartment block, then cuffed and paraded them in front of all their neighbours in an attempt to shame them. Cedar and Lake remained silent, as did we while diligently watching because we all knew getting cuffed was better than a starlight tour. We didn't want the cops to take us, or Cedar and Lake, outside the city limits and leave us there to die.

We mended Star's wounds when she was trans-bashed at the straight bar on Dewdney Avenue after she threw a drink on some assholes who were messing with her and they chased her into the DJ booth, boots first. Afterward, we snuck in through the back of the Club on Broad Street, the only gay bar in Regina, which you had to sign into because there was still a risk of getting gay-bashed. You gained membership by having two up-to-date members vouch for you. The older generation would tell stories about when the local cis-hets drove by in their trucks and chucked beer bottles at the "queers" outside the gay bar.

The Club had changed hands over the years but had been a fixture in Regina's gay community since at least the 1980s. Though it's mostly for the bois now, and it already was back then too, the backbone of that place has always been the trans women and drag queens who ruled it. The local drag scene would still get fishy every Saturday night, and the reigning queens would don their crowns, miraculously affixed on hair "higher than God," as they would say, and brightly coloured rhinestone dresses—perhaps a nod to our country roots. No one stepped out of line at their bar. I remember when an auntie kicked me out of the Club on Halloween when she caught me smoking weed on her side stairs, the meanest thing she could have done on the most debaucherous day of the year. I sure wouldn't make that mistake in her place again.

When I walked through the doors of that small-town gay bar, I walked into a family, into an exercise in kinship and togetherness. I couldn't afford to lose the allies I had when I'd already lost so many others. The connection is intergenerational, and the older generations play mama, bringing up the younger generations, like me, one bottle of Rev and a $5 drag show at a time. Because they know better than anyone else that when gays hold it all inside it hurts more than the rednecks, and they also know about gay love: that hate can't destroy hate, that you'll kill yourself trippin' on hate. From my prairie queer kin, I learned to surround myself with as much love medicine as I was lucky enough to find.

To the prairies queers still loving and fighting: Live loud, live your truth, or just live for tonight, if you have to. Just live, because we need you so bad, baby.

wîhtikow

I'm no stranger to what the kwe call "the slow drive by" for walking north of 105th Street in Edmonton. I remember officer 3191 of the Edmonton Police Service who beat me up in the middle of the night, mere blocks away from my home, because he suspected me of jaywalking. Warning me when I left that I should be very careful when I told people about tonight.

Sometimes I wonder, what is a prisoner? It would seem sometimes that nîtisânak and I were born into a prison. kohkôsak, or pigs, were never there for nikâwiy, who knew above all the language of survival. Who took a knife to my dad when the kohkôsak weren't there to protect her, to protect all of us. Yet were there to separate us into foster care, institutionalize us. nîtisân who did six months in the pen, denied bail, because he got picked up on a break and enter, and was too drunk to know if he had done what they pinned him for. The charges were later dropped but not before he lost half a year of his life.

What is a prisoner? A criminal? Because sometimes I think criminality is just being Native. Existing, or attempting to continue. I have a photo in my kitchen of my nîtisânak wâkâyôs and mêstacâkan, both children. Sometimes I notice the space in their eyes, black holes that could fill the galaxies between us all. I wonder when I look at it, had the abuse already started? mêstacâkan was the oldest, the protector. He took for each of us a thousand blows too painful to name here because we are not your trauma porn. When you see him on the street now you might roll your eyes, say to yourself things your yt liberal sensibilities taught you never to speak out loud but always to think, like, lazy Indian, drunk Indian, junkie Indian, why-can't-you-just-get-a-job Indian. I want you to know he saved me from a sickness that your settlement brought upon our home. He was rewarded with a state of mind that has been diagnosed again and again. Incarcerated, medicated, institutionalized, then spit out at eighteen onto those streets where you found him.

No one ever talks about the Millennial Scoop, the foster care kids who compose a more substantial removal of Indigenous youth than happened at the height of residential schools. A generation of disconnected youth who leave the system at eighteen utterly dependent on the state, and end up dumped into the street to repeat the cycle all over again. I see the ways society criminalizes men in my family for being under mental duress in public spaces. I don't need to read a verbose paper about the marking of Native bodies in city spaces as derelict, a nuisance for removal from the landscape. I don't need to read another needs assessment about how Indigenous bodies are a "problem" to be dealt with using foster care, incarceration, and hospitalization. Sedated by dependence on the state. Immobile and dealt with. Put in our place. I don't need to drive myself crazy reading all that because it's already here in my family. I already know that if we're talking about prison abolition, we have to consider "problematic people," like sexual abusers repeating abusive patterns that were brought into our communities by the colonizers. It's an uncomfortable truth: we can't abolish prisons and not have a plan for ensuring restorative and transformative community process for those who have hurt.

I want the môniyâwak (yt settlers) to know that when mêstacâkan dies on those streets no one will care. The kohkôsak won't try to find me or nikâwiy; they will call him John Doe and turn up their noses at another drunk, high, dead Indian. They'll call it a day, go back to their homes, their perfect porcelain children, their perfect porcelain partners, and their perfect porcelain lives. That he paid for with his body. Yes, he has a body, and a life, just like the môniyâwak; and his spirit will never find its way home, or mîkiwâm, because of them.

I remember the first time I heard N.W.A. say *fuck the police*. Such an urban neechie cliché but it put to words what the môniyâw-kohkôsak do to our communities; do to disappear our communities. That deep, dark secret no one seems willing to name. When Indigenous Peoples say MMIW, missing and murdered, again and again. Almost as if to dissociate, to make less specific the violence we all speak around. To tell the truth of one of the most prolific sources of violence within our lives: the cops, the pigs, the wîhtikowak.

The thing about the cops is, they're all fucking assholes. There is no such thing as the good cop (or the one bad seed, for that matter). They are part of a singular ethos. Cops embody a specific, insidious colonial masculinity. They're the creepy dude you wouldn't go out with so he told everyone you blew him in his car. Of course, they believed him. Why wouldn't they? He was a yt man and you were not. They're every guy who said, "Come on, baby," after you had said no, and the ones who kept going anyway. Cops are Indian agents. Cops are violent johns.

Cops are bullies. Cops are rapists. Cops don't protect us.

Those cops are unruly wîhtikowak, indeed. It's the wîhtikowak who drive nîtisân(ak) to outside the city limits, and make them earn their ride back. It was wîhtikowak who would stalk and harass nîtisân, to intimidate her, let her know not to get any ideas, not to tell anyone what they did to her. Because a wîhtikow could make you disappear, vanish. Those dark secrets whispered among only the deepest of kin: Why do you think they don't want to investigate the disappearances? Stories of starlight tours given to children, bois and girls, women, men, and 2spirit, alike—spread by the ones who returned.

Those wîhtikowak truly are soulless creatures. They eat human flesh and drink the blood of my kin. They laugh at Indigenous pain, and are all too happy to lead Indigenous Peoples to their maker. They are cannibals, part of a colonial sickness that attempts to wane my spirit every day. But, as Chrystos once said, we're not vanishing.[1] The wîhtikowak can keep us on the precipice, teetering between life and death, extinction and resurgence, attempting to remove us from the land before the next generations rise to swallow them whole, and still we rise.

nika-mâci-waniskânân. kohkôsiwikamik nêma ta-nipahi-kwâhkosowak. wâpiski-kôhkosak nêhi. ta-nisîhkâci-kîsisikâtâwak.

BRB B2B:
All the Places We Called Home, Then Burned

The past is a grotesque animal and in its eyes you see how completely wrong you can be.
—*Of Montreal*

12th Avenue and Rae Street, Regina

B2B and I fell in love in the wintertime. I guess there's something romantic about winter in the prairies. Everyone dreads December's bitter cold and seems to fall in love in the summertime. But I think winter is beautiful. All you need is a good down coat—alternatively, multiple layers thrifted (or lifted) from Value Village—then you're walking through the frosted trees and empty streets with their glittering snow that somehow absorbs and muffles sound, and crunches as you walk along it. Such a familiar, comforting quiet, for a prairie kid like me, who has survived many a winter in minus forty weather.

I fell for B2B when they leaned in and kissed me for the first time outside of a party, as snowflakes floated and fell in the air around us. Just like me to fall into a pile of blankets in early December and not emerge until February. They turned the lights low that first night, and everything had an orange glow. I had only ever bottomed, never topped, and started rubbing them like in the videos I watch. They smiled that generous smile that always made me swoon, gently embraced my hand, slowed my pace, and fixed their eyes on mine—pulling me into them.

I moved in with them only a month later, U-Hauling, as the lesbians call it. Thus, my first lesson in love commenced. I would learn to let love simmer, to give it space and let it grow because you never know when the same smile that made you swoon will swoon another, and another, and another, into the bed you share, unbeknownst to you.

This story is the beginning of the end and a reminder to be gentle with my fat, brown, baby-queer self. B2B gave me that first taste, a little nip of freedom cascading out from between my legs, that first rush of water, as plentiful as the ocean, as forceful as its waves, and as sweet as anything I've ever felt. When we were in the throes of love I used to tell B2B that I could never understand breakup songs because I had never been heartbroken, except for after brief flings and puppy love. I think I finally understand what Feist meant when she said that *the saddest part of a broken heart isn't the ending so much as the start.*[1]

97th Avenue and 105th Street, Edmonton

We didn't last much longer in that tiny prairie town before we bolted. Downtown Edmonton was the first place we landed. We found a home in an eighth-floor bachelor apartment that was part of a Boardwalk complex and had a view of the River Valley. Later the locals would tell me it was a "rough" neighbourhood, but to us, it began as a lovers' haven. What's rough, anyhow. Poor? Black? Brown?

We would light coffee filters, throw them off our balcony, and watch them float away into the sky as they burned up. We'd lie in our bed for days, binge watching *Six Feet Under*, smoking weed, and drinking wine, to trip out on existentialism. I'd read to them from my favourite English lit fems, a time before I knew about intersectionality: Zelda Fitzgerald, Sylvia Plath, and Colette. They'd read to me from books that terrified me—*When Rabbit Howls* and *The Heart Is Deceitful above All Things*—and books that, even at my early stage of politicization, I knew were yt boi nonsense such as *Siddhartha*. But I'd try to at least be understanding. We desired only to bask in every last detail of and feverishly consume the other, along with everything that lay within, at the expense of having jobs or money. We spent countless hours there, in that River Valley apartment, dreaming about future lives we were confident we'd share—the travels we would undertake, the children we'd have, our wedding, and the apartment we would make a home. I'd put on Uffie and Justice, pre-Ke$ha Ke$ha, and dance around the apartment barefoot for them, because nothing felt sexier, cuter, better than when they gave me that look.

The rabbits told of the unravelling, though. At least a dozen stencils of rabbits, spray-painted red all over the concrete posts in the parking lot of our apartment, which I had to pass as I left the building. I knew immediately the design was based on our albino rabbit with a bad leg, who my partner adored, and that it was the lesbian housepainter artist who had installed them. I'd never seen any of her art, though. Perhaps she could better be described as a lesbian who lived artfully, by donning that perfect lez-bro hipster style right down to the shaggy haircut, ironic thrifted T-shirt, skinny jeans, and remnants of paint on the hands. She looked like a clone of her girlfriend, who was also a lesbian housepainter. Yt masc queers are always having sex with their doppelgänger, but never brown fems. No one desires that which they are convinced doesn't exist—not even ourselves.

The purpose for the rabbits was twofold. They were a proclamation of love, and an act of psychological warfare, just like the obsessive back-to-back phone calls and showing up at our apartment to continually ring the buzzer when we didn't pick up. Once, when B2B wouldn't answer her, she showed up at my friend's house, where she knew we had just dropped mushrooms, only to mutter strange obsessions and oddities at me under her breath about how she had so much shit on me, and how I was keeping her and B2B apart. It was my first experience of provocation into fem hate and competition. Creator taught me a lesson during those long months, when the painter was sniffing around.

I don't hate the painter. In retrospect, I know cheaters and liars don't tell the truth to anyone, not even themselves. I'm sure B2B told the painter that I was insane and driving them apart; that I was the only thing standing between them. Just like B2B pleaded with me that the painter was a psycho and a stalker, and that they had never loved anyone as they loved me. That's a red flag, dear fems: if your boi calls their date a psycho—ding, ding, ding!—they might just be an asshole.

These are the stories we never tell about lesbian communities because somewhere along the way we convinced ourselves that women couldn't perpetrate violence against other women. In actuality, my most scarring mindfuck relationships have been with folks who identified as lesbians. But, systematically, just like all the times to come, I would forget the painter's name on B2B's lips, her lips in B2B's mouth, and B2B's tongue on her clit. If only I had known then what I know now, like *players only love you when they're playing,*[2] for instance.

I won't say that devotion never wavers, stoking desire as it breathes fire to flesh. There's a poem scrawled in one of the journals I've written in over the years—the first appearance of nisîmis.

I don't even recognize my own life.

My head is empty; and

the heart knows not what it wants.

Green eyes, freckle faced.

You move me...

my socially awkward

baby.

She smokes clove cigarettes.

She confuses me.

I thought I could love her; that maybe she would be something that I was good at.[3] But we were a bit star-crossed. It would still be years before my B2B would set me free. Life is just a series of choices we make, the possible outcomes for which are limitless, and now we'll never know.

I'm sure it seems like I'm having a Jenny Schecter, *Lez Girls* moment.[4] I saw the talking, laughing, loving, breathing, fighting, fucking, crying show[5] in my early twenties, and my friends and I would laugh at it. We didn't know yet what clichés of ourselves we were about to become.

Bethnal Green, LDN

I moved around in KKKanada for several years, not a drop left in my tank but still moving B2B's dead weight[6] trying to find a niche between Edmonton, Montreal, and Regina. Nowhere ever stuck. I kept getting this sense, well it's hard to explain, but, like my life was over. One tends to waste so much time on fatalism in one's twenties. It must be that youthful ego meeting the never-ceasing forward motion of late capitalism. I spent every penny I had getting us to the UK so we could run away, in perhaps a desperate attempt to save us by removing us from the lesbian drama that weighed down on our relationship in Edmonton as a heavy reminder of B2B's past indiscretions. I had even spent a month back out in the oil camps, depressed, lonely, and stir crazy, isolated out there again with the rig pigs. But I did it for us. And, along the last line of thought, I did it to save us.

PRAYER 5 is for the rambling women,[7] who wander to know they're still alive.[8] In LDN when you go out you are in a club with thousands of people, and you leave to a street swarming with millions of animated people. You are no one, except who you want to be at that moment. There's a freedom in that kind of anonymity. It was the real rat race in LDN though—whether you're on your Saturday night search for K, or at your working holiday visa job the following Monday delivering flyers in the LDN suburbs and getting paid for how many you give out. And we were going to give it a go.

Our flatmate would throw parties that would go on until 8 a.m.; there were always lines of coke everywhere. I remember one in particular. *It's Blitz!* had just come out, and Karen O told us to get our leather on at least a dozen times that night.[9] I mostly watched the commotion and rolled joints, everyone coughing, sputtering, and swearing at me under their breath because weed is generally rolled with tobacco in the UK.

Funnily enough, my flatmate was an uptight yt girl with a reserved demeanour and presentation from Saskatoon, Regina's sister and rival city, who I met on Gumtree. She and her Columbian friend were drilling me about my nationality that night. When I told them that I was "Native to KKKanada," my roommate's friend responded, "Oh, a redskin," and laughed—as if he didn't believe me. It was my first realization that in the UK, people genuinely think that we're all extinct. You're not just wrecking with colonial affect—it's imperial, it's the colony too.

Later that night (or morning I guess), a well-spoken bloke from Nepal tried to convince me that racial slurs have no stigma in LDN because of its "melting pot" status. He was quick to throw down about chicken shops later on in the conversation though, his family owning one. The topic of chicken shops is contentious in England because they are primarily migrant owned by folks also on their real LDN struggle. When I was in LDN, yt British folks, well, the conservative chavs and capitalists that is, tended toward a xenophobic rhetoric and were increasingly engaging in identity politics that denounced the presence of migrants in their England, and thereby denounced chicken shops.

The person of colour relationships you forge to survive in suffocating ytness are a minefield of dynamics, the intimacies for and intricacies of which began generations before the moment said relationships form. We all hold the capacity to harbour sensitivities about the stereotypes we've waged war against throughout our lives, while subtly lacking the empathy to be self-critical about the stereotypes we've internalized about others.

Sometimes my mind was active in LDN. Hearing the city through my bedroom windows inspired me to write— the cars in the street, several types of music playing, each fighting in my eardrum for a distinguishable tune. I would begin to think, *It has finally happened for me, I've fallen in love with a city.* But then I would find myself ridden with homesickness. No one tells you how hard it is to be an NDN abroad, removed from your territory for the first time. I missed the friendly banter with strangers who didn't almost push me under the train trying to get a good seat on the Tube. I missed being seen, even if it was the wrong ways, back home, because at least then you know you're alive—British yt folks are ready to mark you as an apparition. I think I knew right away that the motherland of my colonizer was no home for me. Alternatively, when B2B quickly connected with their homelands in the apex of ytness, I should have realized that I was too much for them.

Fortingall, Scotland

When we ran out of money in LDN, we moved to the Highlands, taking jobs as housekeepers and bartenders at a hotel call the Fortingall Yew. There are still sensations that evoke memories I wish I could forget from those days. Like the smell of trees in the night—a freshness on the air that still carries with it visions of B2B.

> VISION 7: Nights spent together among the rolling hills of the Scottish countryside. Drunk on the best Scotch that has ever touched our lips, which we lifted from the pub where we work. Somehow, despite everything that has happened, we are still drunk on love, that first queer love that reaches the hidden parts of you. I guess that's why it is so hard to let go. Despite the bad, sometimes it is so fucking sweet. The tenderness I have locked away for survival and I am now learning to give without condition, however naively. I have cultivated with B2B what I hope is a new beginning and kind of survival: thriving through love.

My body holds memories I wish I could forget because, while sweet, they bring with them moments of regret. Two sides of the same coin: falling in love, and the loss of love. Shame because I took B2B back, and back, and back again. I was young, in the throes of my first love and thousands of miles away from home territories. B2B was my first queer home. I swear I saw them trying to pry open that embittered heart. If I were to forget, I would lose my first lesson in love: you are what you love and not what loves you back,[10] which played the day that they finally left.

Padstow, Cornwall

Cornwall was our final stop in the UK, after our summer contract ended in the Highlands. When we first arrived, I remember thinking something utterly pretentious like a person hadn't lived until they'd driven seaside on the Cornwall coast at sunset, while stoned.

I had kept a disposable camera for over a decade that I had taken with me to the UK. When I developed it, I found that all of its film was underexposed except for a few photos of B2B and me on a beach in Newquay, an oceanside town just outside of Padstow that you could get to by public bus. We look happy. I have a copy of *Rent Girl* in my lap, and we have a picnic of Tesco sandwiches and cider we bought for a pound. We never needed much money to have fun. The photos seem like a cruel joke because those were our darkest times.

We were working for a tourism company that owned a seaside complex with restaurants, a pasty shop, and a chip shop. The company put us up in staff housing nearby where we would hole up in our room and watch British sitcoms or read. I remember reading to myself from Tove Jannson's *Fair Play*, about long love that lasts into the twilight years, the slow, reflective quiet of spending your life and sharing space with someone, creative partnerships, and the power of artistic kinship. I romanticized about it being us one day, knowing that it never would be.

When they told me they had kissed one of the women we shared staff housing with, I never asked them how it happened, who kissed who, or if anything more had happened. There are empty spaces that must be respected.[11] I had begged them to *have a heart, have a heart,*[12] where they had none, one too many times. There was no fight left in me. I couldn't make excuses any longer. I should have known.

I was lonelier than I had ever been. Away from my home territories, with a lover whose love was failing. A self-proclaimed ramblin' NDN, but somehow still homesick despite finally being on the road. I would listen to Joni Mitchell on repeat, thinking of a prairie horizon.

I'm coming home...
Will you take me as I am,
strung out on another man.[13]

I read to B2B from *Fair Play* the night I found out about their Cornwall side girl: you can never go backward, only forward. Against my better judgement, we try anyway.

105th Avenue and 124th Street, Edmonton

We fled home in an attempt to salvage what trust was left, back to the place that was our last source of spatial comfort. It wasn't two months before they cheated on me with our best friend in our bed. It was a cruel joke, really, because we had decided to be poly by that point, so as not to set them up for failure, they rationalized, and the only rules we had carved out was that we weren't to sleep with our friends and certainly not in our shared bed. At this point they weren't working any longer because of their mental health. I was supporting them financially working a full-time job. I was supporting them emotionally, too. I was keeping them alive. I fed them, cooked and cleaned up after them, and bought their Lucky 7 beers, even after I found out they had cheated on me again.

I found out about B2B cheating when I was in Regina for Christmas, without them, and they butt dialled me during the act. A tragic comedy, indeed. When I arrived back in Edmonton they had taken all of my prescription medication. For Christmas they had gotten me a bottle of Sofia, a pink sparkling wine from Francis Ford Coppola's line. The wine was named after his daughter, who was my favourite director at the time. When I arrived home again, it lay empty on the living room floor. Fitting, considering that movie was about the tragic marks that bad bois leave on the rosy glow of girlhoods.

The wolf always finds the fawn. Crumpled on the floor in front of the door of the bathroom we shared in that last apartment we ever called home, begging B2B to stay alive on the other side. Because, if they released their spirit into the cosmos, the last thing I would have said to them is, "I know you're texting that fucking bitch again." The moment I said it, and threw their phone against the wall, I was face to face with nikâwiy. We had stayed together a year longer than we should have, and we just ended up doing terrible things to one another.

B2B submerged their fangs into the very best pieces of my bleeding heart, this nurturing spirit, and sucked until I was dry. I wonder if they feel powerful to have stolen all the very best parts of me? I wonder, if I had ripped my skin apart at the belly button, torn it free from flesh, tendon, and bone, would that have been penance enough? Would B2B finally have seen the way their love burned me from the inside out? Would they eventually feel a smidgen of affinity for the care I had put into everything I did for them, and the fire I kept for them, day in and day out?

nisîmis flew in from Montreal for New Years. We dropped mushrooms and walked through the glinting snow to get away from the black hole that remained in our apartment, that dead weight that was uncritically demanding emotional, mental, and physical output from the only two fems of colour in their life, as they had always been. nisîmis told me that night: "You can leave, you're not stuck, you have options, we make family where we go, you can start all over again—come, to Montreal." I began to believe that I could.

I'm embarrassed to say I stayed even a few months after that, when they assured me we could salvage what was left, until they skipped out to Maryland for a rando yt girl they met on the internet only months earlier. She had that kind of hair only yt queers can: a perfectly straight black bob with choppy bangs. Nothing like my Oji wave, which is probably more of an Oji frizz, to be honest. Her blog was better than mine, too. That perfect mid-2000s blend of ironic html editing, and loaded with pictures of herself in lacy underwear and bratty baby grrrl poses. They left the day before I was supposed to go to court to face officer 3191 who had assaulted me in the street a year earlier, a facet of the normalized culture of racialized police violence toward Indigenous women within the Edmonton Police Service. I was up all night, crying hysterically, and didn't make it to court, an admittance of guilt in the court's eyes.

I'm glad I didn't kill myself the night B2B left, though I came close. I wanted to die because it's the only thing I thought would end the pain. I wanted to be able to see ten years in the future so that I could know that it was worth staying alive. I felt so utterly alone. All I could do was cry, masturbate, and punch myself in the legs—just trying to feel something, anything else but their absence. Well, that and drink. The guy at the liquor store knew me by name. For weeks, it was a pack of Strongbow, a bottle of wine, a tofu cutlet, because I was barely eating, and stalking them online, nightly. I would preoccupy myself by crying over Ikea furniture I was assembling in an attempt to remake my apartment because they had made off with so much of our stuff. I would drill screws into the cheap wood for what seemed like hours, with intermediate cry breaks, single-use l-bar screwdrivers and directions for constructing Swedish-named products strewn around me throughout my empty living room.

Eventually, I felt well enough to go out for a beer with my friend, finally in a space where I could seek out that familiar rush of a heady conversation with an attractive stranger—a primal check-in to see if our pheromones mixed. I saw an old acquaintance, and somehow she ended up telling me about the guitar that B2B gave her. Just like that, I was right back in the thick of the mess they left. I was doing okay, too, finally loosening the grip of their talons. Then I stepped on another landmine they left for me, another lie they told me that they hoped would never be uncovered. I knew exactly what guitar she meant—the one my mom had given me as a teenager, which they had convinced me that our neighbour stole.

My mom had bought me that guitar for my fourteenth birthday. It had been such an ordeal. She didn't understand why I wanted one to begin with, or why I wasn't into more feminine things, like jewelry and makeup. I pleaded my case for months, begging my parents any time we would walk past the guitar section of our local store. When she finally gave in, I remember being elated, like maybe she was beginning to respect my autonomy and voice. I carved *Zeus* into the back, the name I had hastily given it. Everywhere I moved throughout the years, I always had it in tow.

When the acquaintance told me they had given my guitar to her while I was out of town, that time I went to the oil camps before we went to England, to make a little money for us to boot, even though they knew what it meant to me, the veneer finally lifted. They had explained it all away so well for years, convinced me that they were the victim. There was always some extenuating circumstance that made it not their fault—all the other girls were crazy, this is what passion feels like, and a chorus of other half-truths to keep me placated. Worse still, that they were too crazy to deal with any consequences, boundaries, or requests for mediation following their indiscretions. They had used their mental illness for years as an excuse not to be good to me, for hurting me and absolving their own guilt for hurting me. Mental illness is real, but I don't know a single person who isn't crazy and hurt, and we still attempt to be responsive and responsible for the ways we hurt others, at least where it's manageable.

All of that disappeared in that one moment, as quickly as they had left for Maryland. And there would be other lies to come out of the woodwork in their absence, too: other women I didn't even find out about when we were together. This person didn't care for me, at least not in a way that resulted in mutual love. I had made a home with a sociopath and a liar who didn't see my worth but wanted to keep their hold on me nonetheless.

I finally saw the abusive patterns when reading *The Revolution Starts at Home* years later. I had given everything to this person, supported them financially, emotionally, and unconditionally through years of transformation and upheaval. I birthed worlds for them, planned years worth of youthful rambling for them, down to the most minute detail. I had tended to their every sensi-boi need and was the best surrogate mom anyone could have desired. But love, love, love—they wouldn't know it, if it hit them,[14] and it did. My love is so good that it'll lift you to the moon and back. But it's not an obligation, and I feel sorry for anyone who ever took it for granted.

I don't want them punished. I don't want them isolated. I don't want to enact carceral cultures, make myself a cop, judge, and executioner. I'm not here to spread gossip that actually stems from my own ego and reaction to feeling unsafe. I don't want to "name my abuser" just to see them dragged through narrowly defined accountability processes that might kill them. But B2B can stay tf away from me, tbh. Thank Creator for all the unworthy bois who fell back.

105th Avenue and 124th Street, Edmonton, Take 2

They called me on the phone after it was all over. We made small chat. I told them that two books I ordered toward the end, in one last desperate attempt to salvage what was left, had finally arrived after being caught up in customs for months: an eighties edition of *Lesbian Couples* and a book about loving someone with autism. Even though they were never diagnosed, no matter how hard they tried to be, they just "identified with it" (see also: appropriated it). The same way they lifted symbols and spiritual practices from eastern religions—using people of colour as a carte blanche of props to validate their yt, western experience.

"But it's a moot point anyway," I said.

"It's not!" they exclaimed. "I'm leaving Maryland. I'm coming back home."

I couldn't help but smile to myself. Their Maryland lover had seen through the veneer much quicker than I had.

I replied, "Actually, yes it is," rinsed, and repeated every successive time they tried to convince me otherwise.

Sometimes I would just walk around the apartment because it felt so truly mine. It reminded me of my first apartment in downtown Regina, when I would dance around barefoot and listen to Magneta Lane. Everything they made off with when they left actually ended up being an exorcism of their spirit from that home because everything that remained was either unmistakably mine, or something I had made and brought in to create the new apartment. When they came back to Edmonton a few months later sniffing around for what they selfishly, and mistakenly, thought they still had a stake in—that apartment—there was no way to bend the truth this time. This place was mine, and mine alone. This was a life that I had built with or without them.

I would blast Drake[15] on maximum volume, for all the times they shamed me for listening to hip hop and RnB because of their indie rock snobberies.

In a pinch, I threw on my *Back to Black* vinyl. Sometimes, when I was really drunk on red wine, if I sang loud enough,

> it's PRAYER 6 *for a generation of fems fed up with* *toxic masculinities.*

> *I cannot play myself again* > *I should just be my own best friend* > *Not fuck myself in the head with stupid men.*[16]

I took my body back from B2B, as well, for all the pain they had inflicted on it—in similar ways to how I would mark my body with tattoos and dye my hair to take it back from my mom in my youth. In the throes of love B2B and I had gotten couple tattoos based on *Hedwig and the Angry Inch*. Specifically, a song called "The Origin of Love," an ancient queer proverb. As the story goes, folks used to roam the earth with four legs and two faces, and there were three sexes then—the children of the sun, earth, and moon. The Gods grew scared of humans and Zeus split the children down the middle with his lightning bolts. Love, then, is the act of trying to put ourselves back together by making love with someone whose pain is the same, deep down inside. B2B and I had tattoos of the human figures that had been split by Zeus, one half each, and complete when we were together. After they left, I made an appointment to change mine to be the full figure, before Zeus broke it down into two.

Dear fem: I hope you're not disappointed. I know you came for a love song. You want me to romanticize about the power of finding queer love in a small prairie town: finding each other among all the cowboys, truck balls, and hate; falling so fast in love, it didn't feel like falling at all; and laughing so hard the first time we fucked I tumbled out of bed and onto the floor because I didn't know it could feel like that. You want me to tell you about how it felt like ecstasy—like I wasn't entirely alone. You want me to tell you about happily ever after, about love prevailing, romantic gestures, and forever homes. Unfortunately, I have to be the one to break it to you—not all love is for keeps. Take it from me, being in love means sticking around when they're down and out, not when they can't stop cheating on you and tear you apart inside every day, just because one time you told them you would probably stay no matter what they did because you love them so much. Just because they can. Your ex-lover is dead. But *live through this and you won't look back.*[17]

Bottoming

My first queer experience was also coincidentally the first time I was ever topped. Her name was Emil, and she was Chilean. It feels pertinent to mention that because looking back, I recognize her desire was so much more advanced than mine. Though I was admittedly queer and came out as "bi" when I was seventeen to a few close friends, I still naively worshipped the yt queers around me. Emil had already felt that heat of hands running down thick thighs, tongues searching in ways that the thin-lipped yt bois we made out with behind the Exchange never could.

We were at our mutual friend's house, hanging out in her basement with a group of friends, when Emil pulled me into the washroom without warning and pressed me up against the wall. Her hand effortlessly flew to my jeans, which she unbuttoned almost as quickly as she had pulled me in. I was frozen, but I didn't stop her. I wanted her to continue taking me over, taking control. I couldn't think, which surprised me because I'd had a paranoid brain ever since I reached puberty, and my thoughts were increasingly frantic. I could barely catch my breath. I finally understood what it meant to have a spinning head, which was throbbing with the sudden rush of intensity. It wasn't the only thing that throbbed. My mind was blank and I was wet. I knew then I would probably chase that feeling for the rest of my life.

My second time was with pihpihcêw. I had misjudged her as a straight yt girl. To be fair, she was married. But her husband was in jail. I have to admit, I still had a lot of internalized misogyny then and believed that you could tell if someone was straight if she had long blonde hair and dressed in low-rise jeans and tiny, pink T-shirts. I was also still pretty in the closet to everyone but my closest friends. But pihpihcêw sniffed me out a mile away.

We were walking down 13th Avenue in Regina in the dead of winter when she turned to me and said the sexiest thing anyone ever had: "I'm going to fuck your brains out when we get home, and there's nothing you can do about it." My stomach became queasy and all I could do was giggle because my whole body was shaking and I had to focus on it to continue propelling it forward.

Fuck me pihpihcêw did. She fucked me, and fucked me, and fucked me, and made me beg to be fucked some more—all on the floor of my first apartment on Hamilton Street—because that's what a little slut like me deserved. She worked it out with that cheap pink silicone double-sided cock that I bought from one of those grimy adult stores on Albert Street with the boarded-up window—but never once shamed me for having it. That's the kind of tender-daddy she was.

You'd never know what a mean daddy she was to meet her—mousy in the streets and a hard top in the sheets. I guess there were signs, like when she barricaded the door to her apartment when she feared her ex's sister would kick it in that night and I was afraid because her ex kept calling from jail. She had that riff-raff, hard fem sensibility that made a girl feel safe. Or when she cleaned my entire apartment, and then trained me to keep it clean through a cleverly devised reward system. Okay—there were a lot of signs.

When I came out as a lesbian to my dad, he said, "But you've had sex with men before." After pihpihcêw, there was no doubt in my mind that I was A LESBIAN—no more of this bisexual indecisiveness—I was picking a side. Of course, I didn't know about biphobia yet, how love knows no colonial gender binary, that I was actually culturally trans (colonially non-binary), and that intimacy has nothing to do with someone's genitals. I was still a bb queer.

My father's suggestion that I couldn't possibly be a lesbian because I had had sex with men before proclaiming myself as such felt like a childish attempt to dismiss my sexuality. As he believed, I wasn't actually a lesbian, because of my ability to fuck cisgender men. Therefore, the lesbian feminisms I was trying to express to him—newfound conceptions of lesbian ethics, life, and love that were flourishing in my life—were nothing more than raving man-hating. And how could I hate men, he was suggesting, if I have fucked men?

Indeed, I have fucked men. I've loved men, too. I raised the men I loved, from infant to king. I let them suck my holy bosom, this street-smart style, matched with equal poise and grace. I was Creator and Creation all at once by giving birth to them. I gave them life.

I'm an emotional bottom, too. Bottoming is a skill. Knowing how to be tender, how to draw the emotion out, when to tease to get what you want, when to be coy, how to be delicate with the fragile ego, and the exact moment to drop to your knees—remind me again who is in control?

VISION 8: pihpihcêw

i.

That fucking hair
of hers.

It always creeps up on me.
Golden and smelling of jasmine, glinting in the sun,
at dawn, when I did acid and it started raining
    when the drugs kicked in.

Her,
and *that fucking hair.*

ii.

I smoke as ceremony, and smoked long before I
    knew what ceremony was.
Cheap rez cigarettes.

I smoke, much unlike the good NDNs who lay
    down only the best tobacco.
#MoreNativerThanYou[1]

I smoke smokes that you buy on the side of the
    highway, sold in plastic bags.
Buy 100s for $10 a bag.

I smoke the same rez cigs for months, and store
    them in the freezer to keep.
Because I'm poor as hell like that.

I smoke to pull that sweet tobacco into my lungs,
    and feel it cleanse me the way city NDNs like.
Like a fucking meteor.[2]

I smoke when the sadness seeps into the bones,
    when it settles in and makes a home.
Like a lonely prairie wind.

I smoke to distract myself from my feelings,
    another dissociative coping mechanism.
Fuck "bad" coping mechanisms.

I smoke when I start having visions of her, crying
    and blubbering to someone.
Another cliché first love story.

I smoke and say, "I had planned to take her away.
    I could've made it work."
"So why didn't you?"

I smoke and watch the sunrise sitting among my
    self-pity and doubt.
Out there, in the rain.

iii.

Reprieve or obsession?
That fucking hair.

It will come to you in dreams,
sitting on rocks out in the ocean.

You can only see *that fucking hair*,
and never her face.

There are few things I regret more,
than the love I wasn't ready to give.

OG (Kush)

It was love at first (good) trip. Not quite first puff—I didn't get high the first time I smoked weed, after hitching a ride to Moose Jaw to see a punk show with my best friend Jennifer. We had a couple puffs of a joint that was being passed around by the basic punk bros we were hanging out with, but I didn't feel anything (except pissed when one of them told me to stop "skipping in the pit").

The second time I smoked was a different story. I took a couple hauls off of a joint outside of a show at the Buffalo Lounge in downtown Regina. There was a touring band playing that night. As the weed kicked in, I felt as if I was shrinking in size, until I was about two feet tall and the audience and the stage towered over me. This was followed by immediate panic and fear. Because no one told me that your first trip could be so intense. To all my OG babies out there: be careful, do it with someone you love, because your first trip on OG can be terrible. I spent the rest of the night telling my friends something wasn't right, and curling up in a ball in the corner, leaning against Jennifer's shoulder.

Jennifer still hadn't been high yet and was jealous of me. Though my first experience hadn't been great, I reluctantly agreed to find some smoke at our high school, a feat I was certain wouldn't be a problem. We went to

Balfour Collegiate in Regina's inner city. Any innocence we may have brought with us to that school didn't make it past ninth grade. We could pool our lunch money and get a dime bag from any number of stoner bros in the school parking lot, also lovingly referred to as the smoking pit.

I ducked out the doors, hoping not to be seen by any of my yt peers when passing through the school's front foyer. I didn't want them to think I was one of the "crusty Native bitches who hangs out in the parking lot." Of course, in retrospect, those peers were "the suck" (which I wrote in a note to my friend in ninth grade, scrawled in purple ink). But try telling that to the ego of a fourteen-year-old fat NDN grrrl growing up in Regina. The most pronounced racial tension in that city is that between the majority yt population and the Indigenous Peoples who reside (or perhaps are ghettoized) predominantly in Regina's North Central and downtown neighbourhoods. I always knew I didn't belong there, or at least that I shouldn't stand out or draw attention to my racial ambiguity in a school whose sports team was named the Redmen. Maybe that's why I decided to hide behind blue hair.

When we finally scored, Jennifer and I took the city bus back to the east end and smoked inside a garbage bin complex across the street from our old elementary school. My pipe was homemade, rudimentarily constructed from a socket wrench attachment from my dad's tool collection and a plastic screen I had pulled off of our water faucet like my friend had told me about on MSN Messenger. Except as soon as we lit it up, I understood that she had meant a metal screen because the smoke from the plastic made us cough as soon as it hit our lungs—likely why we got so high. I can still hear Jennifer's giggling, so elated she was almost squealing in delight about the powerlines towering over her. It was then that I felt the difference between smoking weed with someone you love in the neighbourhood you grew up in, and smoking at a venue where you're hyperconscious of the way others perceive you. Finally, I let myself ease into it. And so, it was love at first (good) trip.

Something else happened that day. I felt my body—a body I had been dissociating from ever since it began betraying me by growing breasts, a stomach, and hips, and by bleeding and tearing me open from my pelvis every month. I still had shame about my cycle then, and annoyance at the pain that accompanied it. Just another NDN bb grrrl disconnected from their moontime teachings.

More specifically, I felt aroused, and from a surprising source. Jennifer and I were crossing a bridge in a little park near the house I grew up in, and she was wearing an oversized band shirt, a plaid skirt referencing oi-punk, a bright red pair of Etnies, and thick black eyeliner—her typical alt-grrrl uniform. The countercultural references spoke to the young music nerd in me. She turned to look back at me, the sun glinting behind her hair as she did, and it was that simple. I realized right away that I was wet. I don't know if the feeling was always there and the OG finally made me feel it, or if the OG had inspired the emotions, but I knew I had a little heart on for her. Our codependence and my inexplicable jealousy of her boyfriends, suddenly it all made sense: I was living a terrible teen lesbian cliché. I had a schoolkid crush on my bad girl best friend. It was just like in *But I'm a Cheerleader,* when Megan said, "Everyone looks at other girls all the time ... I thought everybody had those thoughts," and I asked myself "the question," because I had thought the same thing. *Am I gay?!* I thought I was looking for a Rivers Cuomo when I felt that lustful ache deep in my chest while listening to Weezer, but maybe I was looking for a Courtney Love, PJ Harvey, or Shirley Manson all along.

OG made me feel, besides gayer, less manic—it would become my brain medicine throughout my teens. I don't know if I get crazier as I get older, or if I just get better at identifying and processing my crazy, but since my teens I have had volatile emotions characterized by outbursts if I didn't self-medicate the crazy away. It took me a long while to be accountable to my trauma/tox-masc trigger, as I like to call it. That's right—fems have toxic masculinities they need to be accountable to, too. In my early twenties I drank because I was afraid of seeing nikâwiy in myself, something I had been running from my whole life, though doing so meant I was ironically mirroring her relationship to substance use. Running isn't just about physical space and territory—it's emotional too.

But OG put me in the driver's seat of my emotions and social anxiety. It takes a lot of OG to calm these prairie NDN nerves. OG was a higher mental plane, a closer relationship to my body, and my first vision quest as a fourteen-year-old scene kid desperately grasping onto anything countercultural to break from that which felt so mundane in Regina.

Funny, I would run from the prairies for decades but always end up wanting to go back. I had to run away to desire remaining finally. I guess Paul was right when he told Holly Golightly that she couldn't run away forever because she'd only end up running into herself—in the shitty racist film version of *Breakfast at Tiffany's*. Even though he was misogynist trash who objectified her, tried to trap her, and lifted her identity to write his shitty book.[1] In the book version, Capote left the narrator unnamed so men would project their desires on Golightly forevermore—the first manic pixie dream girl whose primary role was to support a man's inflated ego and to stand in as his muse. More accurately, a would-be lover a male creative sucked dry like when F Scottie stole all his material from Zelda's journals, then became eternal, whereas she went into a mental institution for not giving a fuck. Like Kahlo and Rivera, Mendieta and Andre, or Claudel and Rodin. It's an archetype, a lesson to never let the male ego overshadow your power if you can help it.

> *PRAYER 7 is for my medicine. There was a tenderness to getting your smoke ready: grinding, rolling, running your tongue along the glue on the paper, perfuming the air, or maybe delicately cleaning then packing your bong. There are so many different ways to get high, getting everything just right for your little five-minute self-care moment, your small pocket of self-love for the day. You could integrate fem aesthetics into your daily weed ritual, using pink and purple papers and sparkling bongs; or amping up the high-fem-bottom stakes, where your lover lifts a different pipe for you each week from the head shop where they work because the owner is a fucking misogynist who never pays enough.*

As I grew, my relationship with OG grew. My first intimate relationship with a plant was with OG, as ritual, revelator, and friend. It was the first medicine I had a daily ceremony with, even before sage and sweetgrass.

Pillz

Weed was a point of tension with my parents, who figured out I was smoking by going through my bags. My parents' carceral relationship to my weed use was always funny to me, because as my mom progressed in her illness, I began to wonder where self-medication started and addiction to numbness began—something I would consider myself much later in therapy after ten years of chronic OG use trying to calm my nerves.

Not everything was so gleaming—all those material things she cared about so much. I knew that while they were searching my room for weed, oxycodone and morphine never ran dry in that house, a seldom-questioned habit she developed in the later years of her illness. But what was the line, I wondered. What made my medicines dirty and depraved, and hers an understandable escape from pain? We all have pain, after all, but seldom have empathy.

I didn't realize that my mom was a painkiller addict until I was in my late twenties. She hid it so well—or perhaps we just normalized it. When I did, it was almost like an epilogue scene at the end of the movie, like in *The Rules of Attraction*, where the director revisits scenes throughout the film that now make sense with the most recent revelation in mind.

My family created a whole language around her illness, which never once addressed the issue of her addiction. We never mentioned how she would scam her pharmacist for drugs she didn't have a prescription for, using the knowledge and institutional (see also: yt) privilege she had gained as a nurse. There was no acknowledgement of the fact that she had this pharmacist on speed dial. We didn't talk about it when she would get so snowed during the day she would pass out mid-conversation, sometimes on the phone, or call me, incoherent, when I was in class.

My dad once told me that he had to do an "overhaul" on my mom's medications, and how she had all kinds of medicine she didn't need. I thought he meant she had been prescribed medication that wasn't necessary to her healing, by quack doctors. I now realize he meant she had opioids that she shouldn't have.

Why didn't anyone save her? Her family, including me? Or the doctors and pharmacists who enabled her? Why didn't just one person speak up? Sometimes I think we just watched her wither away.

The person my mom was toward the end wasn't the person she always was. She told me she always wanted me to remember her "as she was," as if she was ashamed of what she had become. Maybe that's why she was so cruel. Later I would find out opiate addiction makes you erratic and irritable, the way she was toward the end when I was running from her home. Oxycodone eats away at the mind, and prolonged use makes you cruel and progressively dissociated from the world. Same—dissociated, that is, when I was a teen. It was a volatile mix.

By the time she died, she was completely immobile and housebound—which must have been difficult for her to deal with, having been the kind of person who obsessively made lists and worked her way to a nurse educator position at the biggest hospital in Regina by the time she was thirty. It would be an anxiety she would project on me, at times maliciously trying to control every detail of my life as an outlet for the lack of control over hers. I was too young to be patient, generous with her and her illness. I was just a kid, a kid who ran.

I hold many dear memories of my mom. There was always love. But my mom's illness weighed on my entire family. I know I'm supposed to be all neoliberal and exclaim, SHE FOUGHT AND SHE SURVIVED. The truth is a chronic illness that lasts over a decade is fucking hard, and we fought with and survived each other, for a time.

I've seen addiction from both sides now. nîtisân's addiction to crystal meth. The cruel things he did for money like beating up my brother and doing a break and enter on his house. The way he would waste away into a shell of a human and I would worry he would just slip away. And my mom's yt suburban addiction to opioids, from which she arguably did slip away. As weed becomes legal in KKKanada, what remains illegal is use of non-prescribed meds. There's a particular kind of bravado that comes with threatening to call the cops on your Indigenous child because they're holding weed. A bravado tied up in The Truth of the yt man, and an ideology that drug use is only illegal, wrong, and immoral on the prairies if it's done by class-poor brown and Black people.

Feminine Divine

1.

My first interaction with the feminine would be through yt femininity. Old videos from when I was a kid are a record of the fact that my mom dressed me as she would have a doll. In sailor dresses, patent leather Mary-Janes, white frill socks, and a little sailor hat. Dresses upon dresses upon dresses, in all sorts of patterns—polka dot, striped, tiny birds, plaid—all in that same little-girl cut that was tight around the torso and then protruded out from the waist in a mess of crinoline, tulle, and polyester.

I can remember being nine years old on my way to a birthday party and feeling the itchy crinoline under my dress. I was fidgeting and reaching under my skirt, which made my mom spin around to scold me and readjust the crinoline. It didn't matter that I was uncomfortable because at least I looked proper. I arrived at a room full of little kids in dresses, a congregation of living dolls, right down to the curled hair, french braids, and pigtails. We represented our respective moms' success. Our bodies were a place to display both the quality of our mothers' wealth and to adhere to cold war era values about femininity and domesticity. Culture came and went through Regina five

to ten years later than the regular cycle, so suburbanite
Martha Stewart-esque obsessive homemaking culture lin-
gered in our house.

Above all, my mom knew how to keep a home. She
was part of the last generation of real homemakers, who
defined their lives based on the quality of the spaces they
created—a bona fide Joan Crawford. The first thing people
judge you by, she would tell me, is your front entrance,
and the next: the cleanliness of your bathrooms. She had
that classic sense of style, bathing our house in varied
shades of grey and green, and somehow making sure it effortlessly smelled of cinnamon and fresh linen. The family
room, the living room, the dining room all flowed into one
another in a perfect seamless design that matched even
our dishes—all claimed through a secret feminine language, her way of naming the domestic spaces she kept
for us, a world she created around us.

But there was a particular pressure in that veneer, in
the gleam of it all, especially when the weight of illness
bore down, muddying the perfect image she'd projected,
creating cracks in the foundations of her happy home. My
mom was also well versed in, and perhaps hyperfocussed
on, all the cultural niceties that good people were meant
to perform.

Our final fight was about thank you cards. We had
been fighting for years already, it seemed, about the same
old things. Predominantly because the further I strayed
into my own life, the more out of her control I wandered—
or at least that's what my psychologist said. It was just
like us to get sucked into an argument about something so
mundane. But that was always the issue: it wasn't trivial
to my mom—it defined her. "You don't want to look ungrateful," she'd say.

My first Cree language teacher taught me that we don't say thank you; we put our hands over our hearts and bow our heads respectfully.

Interactions like these always seemed to linger, swarm like a cloud, expose some innate difference neither of us was willing to name. My sticky brown fingers were ever finding their way into her porcelain cookie jar. She would slam the lid shut on my fingers, reminding me that I was hers—signed, bought, and paid for—and so too was my body, my embarrassment, and my protruding waistline. It wasn't just the thank you cards, which were merely an object on which to finally project all of the issues that had been building up since the moment I could think, talk, act, and be.

I was my mom's property and my body was a site for management and inscription of yt femininities. If I was fat, she was fat. So, she'd have my dad search my garbage bins for candy wrappers. If I was ugly, at least in her eyes, she was ugly, which she reminded me while screaming, slapping me across the head repeatedly, and calling me names the day I shaved my head and dyed my hair blue. I had done it to take my body back from her, no longer wanting to be a commodity of that perfect settlement she had built. It was the first time I ran.

I still struggle even to let myself believe that our falling out, her illness, everything that's happened, wasn't all my fault. Sometimes I obsess and wish I could go back and be better to her. Sometimes I feel like a stray dog they brought in who tore up the place and never really bonded. But, ultimately, I was just a kid.

I've known from an early age that I'd need to figure out the parts of femininity that were a ingrained in me by my mother from a young age, the parts that didn't feel good.

Where did my desire for racial uplift at an embodied level, likely influenced by my size and want to shrink, end, and the feminine divine begin?

2.

PRAYER 8 is a fem warrior call. It's a Wild Flag record blaring while you coat your lips in paint to survive a shitty day. It's getting angry and knowing it's okay to say your day is shitty because women say sorry too much and anger makes me a modern grrrl.[1] My friend once said to me, "When you're having a shitty day, just apply a good lipstick." I can attest that it works. It's like war paint. Yeah, fuck fem/masc binaries that reinscribe the colonial gender binary on our bodies, but, damn, respect for those fem sensibilities.

PRAYER 9: For My NDN Bb Girls

A moment of prayer for all you NDN bb girls, women or otherwise.

Sage bundles and good vibes to the air for the rez girls, the inner-city girls, and the street girls; for the sex workers from the east side, the north side, or the northeast side, depending on in which lost prairie city you reside. For you bbs in foster care who always give your caseworkers a hard time. Who would read "White Girl Don't"[1] before the worker would come for an inspection, so your sharp tongues were always ready to let Becky Do-Gooder know exactly how stupid she sounds.

This is a prayer for you vagrant NDN youth who ended up in downtown Regina, hanging out on Scarth Street and Victoria Park in the summertime. For you Indigifems on 11th Avenue strolling the faerie track, who used to cackle outside my window at 2 a.m., taking back space by battle calling into the emptiness of the lonely, cold, and long inner-city winter night.

For Rain and Thunder, who got picked up by dirty Regina cops on public indecency. You were such brave babies, for holding tongues to stay alive (not that it's anyone's fault when you couldn't). The pigs cuffed and left you on the street in the dead of winter as if to display and humiliate you as cars drove by on their way through Regina's grimy city centre of sin, on their way back to perfect, pristine homes on the east side, past the Ring Road, with no safe passage for pedestrians and no way for undesirables to walk in. If the cops even held Rain and Thunder legally, that is. The Regina pigs are the same police force that killed Neil Stonechild when he was only fourteen and then laughed about it on the stand. Now every time an auntie, kookum, or sister views the video of the trial your blood turns to ice because you see the faces of your sons, brothers, fathers, and uncles, and the swine that wouldn't hesitate for a second to murder them and get paid tax money to do it, too. Tobacco down for you NDN baby girls who know not to trust the cops.

This a prayer for you crazy bitches, all you iskwêwak who came from a crazy iskwêw, who is the descendant of a long line of crazy iskwêwak from those dirt-poor areas around Prince Albert, Saskatoon, Regina, and the Battlefords. Crazy iskwêwak are just fem NDNs with sharp tongues and quick wit, who are tough as nails and don't take flack, just like you learned in the spirit of your people.

Burn a braid for your girls exercising your tribal sovereignty on the pole, Instagram, and on the strip. For all you bb girls with that halfbreed, city NDN know-how. As Missy says, ain't no shame baby, do your thang. Just make sure you're ahead of the game.[2] Prayers up for prosperity. Prayers up for getting the cash up front.

Crack a can of Pilsner for your femDNs who know not to get in cabs alone late at night in the prairies. You know all too well that sinking feeling when your taxi turns into an industrial area that you don't rec-ognize—that anxious desire to bail out the passenger door, and the fear it might be child-locked. So instead you organize ride shares at last call. This is what harm reduction looks like, and public health does not prescribe it. It's just a few neechies looking out.

Sing a song for your Indigibabes who make acrylic shine like diamonds, and $10 mukluks that you lift-ed (see also: liberated and repatriated) from Ardene look so good, they might as well have been handed down from the ancestors. Sing for the girlies who walk through city streets with a stride so assured of your ownership over urban territories, as if you have the ancestors backing every single step. For the con-crete roses[3] who see the beauty in the grime and grit.

I see NDN bb grrrls in the street, with your eyes straight forward, headphones blasting, and that don't-fuck-with-me scowl that says to others, don't mess; that shows me that you see me, too. With million-dollar aspirations, and that rez state of mind. Trying to find a little piece (peace) of that sweet love you heard about on that Patsy Cline record kikâwiy used to play on

Sunday afternoons. And love, you will. Your screams of pleasure will call out to the star ancestors, and heal the ravaged hearts of your fem clan before you. Heal yourself, you heal your bloodlines.

This one's for you, all the NDN bb girls, women or otherwise. Your body, your survival, is sacred even if it's grounded to the land through the connection of sneakers to concrete. You're an inner city baby who might not always be okay, on the truth, and re-surgent; who goes crazy, who mouths off, and who needs to self-medicate sometimes; who might not be one of the "good NDNs." But you're still here.

Generations

The Apple Tree

My great-grandmother Stevenson lived to see her ninety-eighth birthday, though her actual presence at the celebration of this day is debatable. My family huddled in her tiny retirement home room with offerings of cake, flowers, and well wishes. We went through our now ritualized process of taking turns talking at my grandma, the cavity of a woman, as she stared vacantly at the ceiling above her. This process was unsettling to me as a child. In the halls outside her room, I could hear the cries of other residents who seemed trapped within the confines of their minds and bodies, and alarm bells rang out through the hall constantly as the residents tripped them because they were in need of a nursing staff stretched desperately thin. Even at the naive age of twelve, I could see my grandmother no longer inhabited this body.

My great-grandmother's funeral was equally upsetting to me. Her skin looked orange and waxy. She was clearly dead, her expression frozen and her body stiff in the open casket, but she was awkwardly reanimated with make-up and prosthetic tricks. Viewing her body made me nauseous. I've never understood the yt, western fascination with preserving the body in morbid and obsessive ways—as if mourning, and death, are undignified, or perhaps the act of going back to the land and being made worm food is what's seen as degrading. Ergo, death, and burial, must be prolonged and put off. The body must be preserved.

When my mom died I refused to view the body before she was cremated and, when presented with the option to see her body by the funeral home worker, I thought back to the unease I had at viewing my great-grandmother's body. My brother B was mad I didn't go into the room where her body was, thinking it my duty, though he came out of the room white-faced and completely shaken. He saw some manly stance in having seen the body. But I didn't need to see her body to know that she was gone. I already felt it.

In one of the few photos that I have with my great-grandmother, we are standing in the backyard garden of my grandma's house under her apple tree, the house where my mom grew up. I couldn't have been more than three. My great-grandmother's hand is gently resting on my back as the other points toward the camera in front of us. Seeing this photo as an adult, I am always caught off guard by the expression on her face. For as long as I could remember, my great-grandmother lived with a kind of monotone and vacant expression. Her animated nature in the photo of us was something I didn't remember seeing before. She had humour on her face, a smile spread from ear to ear, as she pointed to someone behind the camera, likely my grandmother. There was love in her gesture, reaching out and placing her hand on my back, guiding my gaze forward to my grandmother. It's the most interaction between the three of us that I had witnessed since my great-grandmother withdrew into herself and age. This photo of my great-grandmother and me captured a version of her I didn't know. But, from that photo, I can see that her love for me was a love eternal. Though I've lost the feeling of her touch, the sound of her voice in those moments of sweetness, her love is a medicine finely woven into my very being.

PRAYER 10 is a grandmother's sacrifice. Great-grandma Stevenson was at an orphanage, at one of Dr. Bernardo's infamous homes for destitute children. She was one of the estimated 100,000 young migrants sent to KKKanada as a part of the so-called child emigration movement that the Canadian and British governments try to spin now as child welfare campaigns, meant to give impoverished youth a better life than they would have received in London slums. But my great-grandma wasn't from the slums. She was only twelve years old, and my great-great-grandparents sent her to Dr. Bernardo's because they were living on a farm near Crediton in poverty and unable to provide for their youngest daughters. Bois on a farm were currency. Girls, on the other hand, were just extra mouths to feed. Great-grandma was sent to KKKanada at thirteen without the permission of her parents, who sent her to Dr. Bernardo's imagining she would stay there. In KKKanada she was an indentured servant to KKKanada's settler bourgeoisie, and integrated into a home in Peterborough when she was fourteen so she didn't have to go to school. Great-grandma spent the rest of her teens doing housework until she could make a break at eighteen, setting out across the country with "some guy," as she would tell it, settling on a farm near Findlater, Saskatchewan.

No—my great-grandmother wasn't my blood family. But this scrappy spirit and rambling heart are the product of my Red River blood and the country women who loved me, as well. I'm ever suspicious of Indigenous people, especially yt-passing Indigenous people, who never acknowledge their yt relations. Who, what, is being erased and negated? Fuck the performative Indigenous future, political puritan theory grounded in lofty ideas and zero ethical responsibility to our kin in this fucking moment. What about the Indigenous right now? What about the settlers I care for, the ones I love and the ones I have come to call kin?

Last Mountain Lake

My grandma grew up dirt poor. Like on a farm in the middle of nowhere, in hand-me-down clothes made from old dishrags—it's not just a stereotype from Dolly Parton songs. There was a particular kind of isolation on the Saskatchewan plains that bred men who ruled with an iron fist, on farms that no one could reach—not the law, not their wives' families, and certainly no one without their permission. Grandma would tell me stories about her father's cruelty, giggling when she relayed to me the times he would hit her elbows with a knife if she had them on the dinner table and sometimes they would bleed. Things were different then, she'd say.

She never used to hug me and I never held it against her. From an early age, I knew that my great-grandfather's farm had hardened her in ways that I couldn't understand. But somehow she retained enough tenderness to remain the most sensitive person I knew in my early life. The smallest kind gesture would move her to tears. My grandfather would say she cried so much because her tear ducts were too close to her eyes. She was also extremely guarded, only divulging small details about her life to me: that she met my grandpa at a skating rink in Regina, for example, but never with any of the details of the story of their meetings, or how they fell in love. She kept the difficult things from me too, which I would only find out years later through other people. For instance, my grandpa's affair, the physical abuse her sister endured for years, or my grandpa's accidental killing of an older adult when he was a truck driver returning home from a long haul. To grandma, life was a matter of facts with no flourish. And there are just some things that are not to be talked about.

My grandma had Depression era frugality that she carried with her throughout changing times. My grandparents still bathed in the same water, even when they were staying at my parents' house in the city. On the farm, water was hauled in from the well, and even in retirement my grandparents' water source was pumping it into the house from the lake and filling up jugs to bring back to the cabin when they were in town. There was a particular kind of intimacy in these practices: that they continued to share bath water long after they needed to, even though I rarely saw them touch; that, by not putting plumbing into their cabin, they created a need to come into our house biweekly to refill their potable water. They created reasons to bring us closer, where the prairie had hardened their hearts. My grandma had lived through rural Saskatchewan poverty, the hard hand of my great-grandfather, and the cruelties of men, making emotionality sometimes hard to express and now recoiling from the tenderness of touch to express affections. Tasks to keep home and hearth became a way to reinforce the closeness between us all, without the lingering awkwardness of touch.

My grandma liked the simple and quiet of life at the cabin. I remember the slow easy summer afternoons there that seemed to last forever. I would get excited when my parents would turn their van down the gravel road to the cabin and I could begin to smell the beach. As soon as we stopped, I wouldn't waste a second running into the lake, and would proceed to bob around in it all day. We would go out in the winter too, which provided equally exciting moments, like the time my grandma taught me to ride a ski-do. She would tell the story for years after. For practice, she told me to drive up to the turnaround, which was at the top of a hill, and come back. When I reached the turnaround, instead of braking I accidently accelerated and ended up driving off the hilltop, getting thrown off the ski-do in the process. I remember lying winded at the bottom of the hill, having narrowly missed some rocks. But we would laugh at that story endlessly for years to come. What doesn't kill you makes you legend in the prairie countryside. There are some stories you do tell. Namely, the ones that bring joy.

I was once a nine-year-old asshole who read the journal my grandma kept. There was none of the juicy family gossip I expected to find. Instead, she wrote pages and pages about animal sightings and nature walks.

Today I saw a Chickadee when we were sitting on the porch.

We went to the turnaround last night, and there was a deer at the lookout.

We walked up to the ravine today and saw a skunk.

I thought my grandma's journal was dull, the wanderlust having already settled into my bones. I wanted intrigue and secret family drama. I didn't get that she was on that higher plane, that contemplating silence racket, that pleasure in solitude grind, that only grandmas and kookums can pull off. She saw a quiet beauty in the world that my restless thoughts couldn't grasp yet.

VISION 9: I'm running through the grassland fields behind my grandma's cottage in the springtime, picking chokecherries and Saskatoon berries, when I come upon a bush and crocuses, and pick some for my great-grandma who lived under my grandma and grandpa's care for most of my youth. Nevermind that the berries don't ripen until the summertime. My nighttime visions are reserved for all the sweetest prairie feels. I return to the cabin, and to the smell and crackle of the wood-burning stove that my grandpa stoked day and night. My grandpa taught me respect for the water, but simultaneous confidence in my movements when balanced atop her in a boat. She has to respect you, too. My grandparents were the backwoods Saskatchewanian country-folk, whose humility, gentleness, and care for community nurtured this restless spirit, this home on the horizon, as well. But, as runoff brings the shoreline higher and higher each year, and the cabins across the lake from my grandparents' begin to fall into the water, what the liberals call global warming (and I just call global colonialism), I know that land is nature's to take back, too.

East Side, Saskatoon

nikosis was the first-born ôsisimimâw of nikâwiy. Of all the things I want to say to nikosis, the most important is that I hope nikosis always knows he is loved.

I know I should probably wax poetic about resistance, strength-based approaches and body sovereignty as if nikosis's body is his own, as if settlement hasn't corrosively been wearing away at it since the day he was born. I know it's all so much more complicated than that.

I wish I knew how to tell nikosis about who we are as a people, whatever that means, without talking about violence, but I think it's at least significant that I witness him by not pretending that he can think himself out of the daily reality of his life. I'm not going to lie because I respect him more than that. I know whoever we are as a people extends into a deep-rooted culture of shame passed from generation to generation. It manifests itself in all kinds of ugly and abusive ways, both projected on one another and self-inflicted. But how do we even begin to unravel these inheritances, begin to heal ourselves and our bloodlines, without talking about the hurt? And why can't I talk about the pain without being a traitor to the cause?

But, being a small-city, prairie NDN is a proud lineage too.

Pride in the prairie city NDN struggle is PRAYER 11. I hope nikosis knows that. Though we have troubled histories chronically fatiguing us now, fucking with our brain chemistries, our ancestors were warrior

*women, medicine men, and political leaders. We
are here because someone in our bloodline struggled
tooth and nail so we would survive. I want nikosis to
know that his dad, my brother wâkâyôs, was born
and bred in that struggle. wâkâyôs didn't get a lot
of opportunities to be anyone other than who he is
now, and he's been pounding that pavement since
he was a kid, just trying to live to see another day.
The world hardened him. Unspeakable violence always marred our home, a home I escaped from at a
young age, and which would be his first prison. Well,
that and years on the strip making quick cash, foster care, and the occasional bridge in a pinch—what
the yts call poverty, and we just called getting by. I
don't say this to garner sympathy. But I want nikosis
to know that his dad wâkâyôs did what he had to so
that nikosis would come into this world.*

When wâkâyôs looks at nikosis, he sees his own innocence lost in nikosis's potential, and fears for everything
he can't give. He can't imagine how to undo all of the pain
that our parents went through, our grandparents went
through, our great-grandparents went through, and that
we, in turn, went through. He wonders how nikosis's life
will turn out and, like me, he wants to believe that his son
will have every opportunity to be healthy, happy, and provided for. And that nikosis won't experience the abuse itself, any of it, please Creator.

But wâkâyôs knows something that nikâwiy knew
too. It might take years for nikosis to understand and be
able to access empathy—not nikosis's fault, obviously,
because wâkâyôs is the adult. But, just like nikâwiy, he
knows that he has nothing left to give to nikosis, so in a

fucked-up way, it's better if he stays away. Some part of wâkâyôs likely thinks he doesn't deserve nikosis, either.

While we're on the topic, I hope nikosis knows that nikâwiy, kookum, told me the other day, "We come from strong nations," something she had never said to me before, and I cried like a baby. I know that's not the kind of shit prairie NDNs are sitting around and saying to each other all the time.

If there were only one thing I could say to nikosis, it would be that we come from strong nations.

Simple Folk

Skyler never wanted to come with me to visit my aunt (my mom's sister) and cousins who lived on a farm outside of Regina, when we were back home. They felt unsafe: "You even said your cousins were rednecks," they would say to me. "What if they find out I'm trans." Fair. But, for the record, I said it lovingly. I said it in that little bush, country-folk kind of way. That I-know-everyone-from-the-town-over-by-name-and-visit-with-my-neighbours-on-a-regular-basis, bringing-carrots-from-my-garden-and-pickled-eggs thing. That country wild way, living on a farm in the middle of nowhere, where not even the sheriff can reach and even the terrain was as unruly as the people who settled it. Wild weeds and grasses grow with reckless abandon on the farms in the country, unlike the tidy green grass lots that speckled the neighbourhoods I grew up in. Lower-class, unsightly folks inhabit the open, who don't care about wearing a suit and tie to work or how clean their front entrance or bathroom are because they've got farm chores to do. Milk the cows, help with hay baling, get the eggs from the chicken coop; repeat, repeat, repeat.

There's a lawlessness to the prairie farm. I had my first cigarette in my Auntie D's farmhouse with my cousin Wily who always had a hellish side. When he was a young adult he had warrants for running from the cops and was eventually caught with large quantities of drugs. During my teens, I would smoke weed among the hay and cow pies with my cousins at family events, as our parents unknowingly, or perhaps knowingly, socialized in the house.

Perhaps knowingly because they definitely ignored our youthful indiscretions in many cases. In fact, it was my grandpa who had given me my first drink as a pre-teen, slipping me a rye and soda in secret when the rest of the family was sharing a drink.

One of my first boyfriends was a farm boi. He lived across the dirt road from my cousins' farm and he used to drive around in his shitty car blaring a remixed version of the song "Cotton-Eyed Joe." What can I say? When you're a young slut in the prairies, you make do. Well, where you can. A gay boi could have gotten killed making passes at country bois. And that's the other side, isn't it, of the holy country wild. There's the same lawlessness imbued in the right to protect one's person and "property," as well.

After all, it was a good ol' country boi who shot and killed Colten Boushie and got away with it. My grandparents and I would argue much later about what happened that day. "They had guns in the car," my grandma would say, to excuse Boushie's murderer coming at him gun first. Did I ever yell. Like, I've seen shirts at rad queer book fairs read *Fuck your racist grandma*, and fuck my racist grandma, too. Some things you never talk about. But maybe some things you should push to talk about.

There's something wild about being us prairie NDNs, too. My nîtisânak and I were, are, lawless, but in a different way than my yt family. It's hard to explain. Like, there's the city, the yt man's law (The Truth), and then there's NDN law, and the NDN underbelly of any prairie city. NDNs have their own understanding of what is and isn't acceptable, agreed upon between one another, and breaking the yt man's law is almost always acceptable, a means to an end, even. It's knowing which neighbourhood you shouldn't step into because your brother isn't

welcome there so you certainly aren't either. It's pro-
tecting your family with a knife, sometimes. It's groups
of Indigifems taking justice into their own hands by con-
fronting, and maybe even beating up, their friend's abusive boyfriend who hit her and broke into her apartment
to scare the shit out of her because you're pretty sure he
could kill her, and you're both afraid of prairie cops who
rape and kill NDN women. It's all the scams NDNs can
run on the city, in the city, to make a quick buck. Unlike
yt country-folk lawlessness, NDN lawlessness can get you
dead but, at the end of the day, at least you know you're
living the city-sovereign life.

Funnily, Skyler had never taken my concerns serious-
ly when I told him that he and his family's views about
country-folk—uncultured, backward, boring, simple folk,
as they say—were classist and racist, considering all the
NDNs who live in the prairies. When I hear someone talk
trash on prairie folks, prairie cities, and prairie lands, I
just assume they're a classist, racist asshole who I probably don't like anyway. ¯_(ツ)_/¯

For My Descendants

Illustrations by Kablusiak

Portions of this chapter were initially collected for E, as a gift on the day of their coming of age ceremony. kinanâskomitin.

> *PRAYER 12 is for my descendants, for all my 2s kin to come. These are some of the 2s teachings I gathered in my youth: in ceremony, in lodge, from my kin, and on the wind.*

Gwekwaadziwin: I used to live in a lesbian commune, lez haus, we called it, and thought I was living the dream of fourteen-year-old me, who read about lez houses in the gay and lesbian section of the downtown public library, imagining that someday I'd be able to create my very own freak fam. When I finally did get that reality, we mostly just drank too much and were abusive to one another, myself included. I knew dick all about "accountability," I still know dick all about accountability, and was drinking every single night. I didn't know yet that nothing good can be found in the bottom of a 40 of vodka.

We never talked about the abuse though, because we were all "women" (even though we weren't, but we didn't know it yet). Taking a page out of Thirza Cuthand's book, I won't tell you it's okay when your girlfriend gets violent when she's drunk—mainly because I know that intimate partner violence somehow gets normalized within queer communities.

My abuser was 2s and primed me for over a year before they started being emotionally violent. They positioned themself as a mentor through 2s youth organizing and drew me close by validating my gender with spiritual and cultural knowledge. Once they had drawn me in, they started behaving coercively. They would always find reasons I was fucking up—I hadn't shown them proper respect for them by asking to stay at their house when I was in TO, or I had assumed other people's gender by saying I rocked with mostly "non-dudes." The reasons I was fucked up and being punished became increasingly bizarre, innocuous, and random to the point where I felt like I was constantly monitoring my actions and words when I was with them to avoid conflict. When I set a boundary, telling them I needed some space and time, the behaviour escalated, only ending after they sent an accusatory email to all of our mutual acquaintances containing our personal email correspondence about some of my most intimate experiences, including outing me as a sexual abuse survivor.

It hurt but I learned some shit. I learned to protect myself. Pull people close who show genuine, reciprocal care for you in tangible and material ways, and return that love. The only people who get angry when you set boundaries are those who benefit from you having none to begin with. Violence is and isn't gendered—queers can be violent too. I know it's so much more complex than kill all men (except, let's be honest, kill all men). Violence is insidious and flows throughout our communities. You can't build trust with someone based on identity alone. And, lastly, a mentor who is punishing isn't a mentor at all.

Dear 2s youth: I witness you. I witness you. I witness you. I witness you. One time for each direction.

Mnaadendimowin: Take care of your body because it's sacred, no matter what the haters say. The cis-hets want you to feel like your dykey body is a disgusting, fat abomination. But I, like Laura Aguilar, know that your body is beautiful and matches some of the most beautiful forms in nature—rock formations that mimic the sturdiness of your frame, and lakes that emulate the curves of your soft rolls. Take care of your body for the land because your body is sacred no matter where it stands. Your body is sacred even if you're an inner-city bb. The city is land, too.

Zaagidwin: Be as soft as you can be (but it's okay if you can't be soft, too). The people you will meet will try to make you hard, because the world is a hard place to live in. But do what you can to remain worthy and true to yourself.

Dbaadendiziwin: Always be kind to animal, plant, and other nature kin. Try to communicate in whatever ways you can. It was Lacie Burning who taught me that non-binary bodies are phantoms on the land, speaking to creation in fluid ways that move between the physical and psychic realms. Extend this power to all your relations.

Nibi is a 2s teaching. Nibi has no gender because it's fluid. Nibi touches and gives to everyone unconditionally. 2s are like nibi: We are honoured to move throughout and within women's and men's circles, and between the olders and youngers. We are a bridge, a median, and an emotionally safe space to do work between all the sections within our lodges. To do this work is an honour.

Nbwaakaawin: 2s urban kin raise one another, and take care of each other fiercely and uncompromisingly. Don't let anyone shame you into thinking your family is wrong because it doesn't look like theirs. Family is fluid, not finite, and you make it as you go along in life. 2s kin will be your teachers, and you'll teach your 2s kin. You will mirror to one another what 2s life is, and create new histories and traditions as you do.

Debwewin: It doesn't always feel great in ceremony when you're 2s. You can be made to feel like you're making a big production when you're just trying to navigate ceremonial spaces in ways that feel safe to you. You deserve to feel safe in ceremony. There are so many people before you who had to do their own thing and carve out their own space in ceremony. You're not alone. If you ever feel bummed, strategize ways that you can have safe ceremony by yourself or with people you trust, even if that's not always Indigenous people. We need to take advantage of kinship and ceremony where we can.

Aakwa'ode'ewin: In the words of Kimya Dawson, *if you wanna kill yourself remember that I love you.*[1] I always loved Dawson's honesty on "Loose Lips," because I was once a teenager dealing with suicidality on the daily. Hearing my idols speak openly about depression and suicidality empowered me, realities I now know emerged from wanting to end the complex, uncontrollable emotions I experienced when I was under mental duress—when I wanted to end the pain. I know what it feels like to go to that dark place, that down low place, where no one can find you.

Where it doesn't matter if people love you because you just want to go to the dark.

But I think you're badass. I think you're on a fantastic path. I think you're going to be such a radical 2s leader for your community, even if just by continuing. I can't wait to see that person you become. You have 2s kin who love you solely because you exist, who want you to thrive and stay alive, so you are never alone. You're awesome, and you're going to keep being awesome with the help of your kin. I love you.

What Artists Have Taught Me

Siqueiros

Sure the muralists were anarchy bros, but I was a young anarchy bro once, too. Revolution can sound rather badass to an insurrecto nihilist NDN youth who wants to destroy the settler-colonial nation-state. Anarchist revolution is always so hyper-mascy, though, as if the rev has no place for women and children, and chaos and violence characterize our natural lawless state. But I know that if the rev came the aunties and kookums would be so bloody organized, so locked tf down, that the warriors would just fall into line, and negotiations and the safety of Indigenous children would come well before camo-clad stoic warriors on the front line.

Still, I was inspired, after having had the western canon shoved down my throat for so long, when I saw *Collective Suicide.* As the story goes, the Spanish conquistadors were invading Chichimec territories, modern-day Mexico. The Chichimec saw that the Spanish armies were stronger than they had ever been before and, this time, they would lose the fight. The entire community jumped to their death off of their beloved mountain ranges, rather than being captured, tortured, and dominated by the impending colonial force.

Sometimes, when you grew up NDN in the prairies, somewhere between fighting to be seen and struggling to blend in, all you need is a potent revolutionary statement from your comrade in the struggle to inspire your budding revolutionary visions.

Miss Chief

Of course, I know it's all so complex now. Why'd Miss Chief have to go and marry Jean Paul Gaultier for all the capitalist daddies at the Beaux-Arts? Why does Monkman lift trans femininity so flippantly, even though he's an affluent cis gay? How is she everything and nothing all at once, a drag queen but not a drag queen, trans but not too trans, and 2s but not a voice for 2s?

Despite my complicated relationship to Monkman's work, witnessing other 2s life was the audacity of queer possibility and desire-coded revolution. Having for so long moved through museums that presented only anthropological representations of the imaginary Indian, through a world absent of other queer NDNs, seeing Miss Chief was revelatory. There she discoed, in all her glory, wearing a fabulous all-red number, a necklace comprising multiple strands of shells exaggerated to a level of supreme luxe indulgence. I was transformed. Such a little 2s dirt-fag cliché, finally, I saw myself, my most authentic and queerest self, on the gallery wall, in aesthetics easily readable and understandable to me. Would I be where I am today if Miss Chief hadn't shown me that I belong somewhere?

In the future I would admire other queer cultural objects the same way I did Miss Chief, like *RuPaul's Drag Race*. I appreciated that these *things* created a secret queer language, an aesthetic, and a vernacular and linguistics indecipherable to straights. Of course, that was also before I understood the problematic underpinnings of culture made for specifically for gay yt men. Give me an unapologetic, loud, boundaried Vixen over a temperamental, mouth-writing-cheques-her-ass-can't-cash Aquaria(us),[1] any day. Thus spoke the light pseudo-religion that is astrology.

Yes, that's a Nietzsche reference. And a Kundera reference, even though Kundera was a fucking asshole. Sry not sry, Kundera. If someone asks to be slapped across the face repeatedly so they can spray cum all over your bedroom floor, the back alley you're making dirty in, or wherever, you better beat the hell out of that beautiful sub bb—if you consent, that is; or if you don't consent, but like it that way.

Fuck these yt bois out here, too light to hold down. When Miss Chief started empathizing with the light, yt bois, making work for the gaze of the yt daddies, I began to wonder if she was too light to hold down, too. I started to wonder if there was ever an ethical etherealness to her fuck, to begin with. But, I guess Miss Chief was always an idea, an apparition, a disappearing NDN. Even though she's a vision of a long lineage of gender-fuck life, maybe she's just a cheap existentialist quandary on ethical love, walking around some French-Canadian city with a Camus tattoo and worn-down copy of *The Unbearable Lightness of Being* in her back pocket—a modern-day Franz.

Malbeuf

I saw Amy Malbeuf's *kayâs-ago* at the Art Gallery of Alberta in Edmonton. I was on a scarcity-driven path to law school, having worked hard to barely survive since my teens and finally worked my way up from a general studies program at the local college into a Native studies department at the University of Alberta. I was taking a Latin American art course at the same time, as an elective for my Native studies major, and I was beginning to understand that NDNs had their own recording devices outside of the written word—the material, our art.

Malbeuf collected quotes in Cree, Michif, and English from people who had influenced her—relations, people she loves, figures of inspiration—and created light installations that displayed them in Cree, Michif, and English. Each letter that composed the displays was painstakingly crafted from caribou tufting. I took a picture of that clichéd Louis Riel statement because I, like Malbeuf, still found some romanticism in it: *My people will sleep for 100 years, but when they awake, it will be the artists who give them their spirit back.*

Malbeuf called her relations, our relations, into the conversation within the space of the gallery. Her caribou hair panels were stand-ins for agential beings, made animate through the kinship ceremony at the centre of Malbeuf's practice that pulls these materialities into psychic connection and relatedness with Malbeuf, the space of the gallery, and the other spirits Malbeuf called forth.

Viewing *kayâs-ago*, I understood that I could be

politically sound drawing from cultural objects, and not just from colonial legal and historical documents like all the masc-bro theory I was reading in Native studies. Malbeuf's light installs are the Métis fem teachings I couldn't read about in theory seminars that are mostly about that Louis Riel, Gabriel Dumont, and whole Red River revolution jerk-off thing (meaning no mention whatsoever of the roles that women and 2s played).

kayas-âgo was a remembering of women's knowledge and kin-making practice, based on the material and the social relations that facilitate love. My people were made with love, not a legal document written in a colonial language that my ancestors were starved into signing. The enforced professionalism and naturalized yt politicking of academic spaces—what Said has called making oneself "objective"—have never been ready for us scrappy, low-class Métis bitches with hot tempers and smart mouths like our kookums.

Danger

I'm going to break from the whole timeline of this book just to give my kwe Danger a shout out. We're the future, anyway. It's like, how many works can I look at that deal with the cultural and visual signifiers of the vanishing NDN—a feather here, a headdress there, a mean-looking warrior type with a gun, or two. Why can't an NDN be fucking, slutty, young, brown, wild, and free?[2] Danger taught me that I'm powerful, even when I'm slutty.

I've been a reluctant academic because I don't believe in individual claiming of knowledge. Indigenous knowledge has always been collective, meant to be shared and generated within a space of mutual thought. Yet, every scholar I know, even if Indigenous, at one point or another has tried to convince me someone has stolen their ideas. The academy breeds paranoia and suspicion—rampant individualism—instead of mutual acknowledgement of the shared aesthetic we generate with our contributions to NDN thought. Collaborating with and thinking alongside artists who brought me into their practice has become a means of refusing individualist thought in my writing and intellectual production.

Enter Danger. Danger showed me how intimate that artist-writer relationship can be. Thank Creator, thanks creators, for giving visuals that inspire writers to put words to paper about aesthetics. Artists seem drawn to the visual because of a struggle to materialize words about their practices. And, thus, the cyclical and dialectic relationship of arts writing is formed. Danger showed me what it feels like to be truly kin'd up, never out there alone with your thoughts. Only ever with strong sibs behind you, in the streets and on the page.

Danger helped me self-actualize that my truth is valid, that my truth is NDN truth, even if the big bois wondered why "everyone is naked" in their work, and called my crit of it "soft talk." It's cool—not like we expected them to understand how political, how fucking punk rock, a lens that consciously excludes them is.

Danger taught me to stay true to my voice even when the haters are coming down because all we have is ourselves. More importantly, to rage with style, humility, and love. No one asked for my side of what happened, that time I got stalked and harassed by the NDN art bros, by ~THE NDN ART BRO~ except my sib, Danger. They were the only one who held me down when they all said, You were asking for it, you're the one who chose this career, oh c'mon, it wasn't that big of a deal.

Danger, thanks for making work that keeps me alive, kwe. Thanks for keeping relational politics that back up the work, that also keep me alive. You taught me never to be afraid to speak my truth in this industry, or else I'll lose my head; but to save my breath, too. Here's my truth. Like most feminized folks, I doubt it will be believed anyhow. So that's all the vultures get.

Epilogue: Tio'tia:ke

This book was PRAYER 1: For me, for nikâwiy, and for my mom. Also, for closure and for my truth, for once. As a ward of the state, my whole life has been constructed for me by institutions. I've felt I'll never be an independent person because so much of my reality has been influenced by the adults around me whose care I was in. To complicate matters, the prairie functions to ensure The Truth, the yt man's truth that is, reigns. I guess that's why I was always running. I was on the lookout for something a little more, something that I thought I'd find in the city. Now that I've lived in cities for a decade, I think I was just called to the horizon, like my rambling kin before me, because now I just dream about going back home, to the rolling hills of wheat. The city still has its gritty charm but I'm a little more jaded, especially about the dirty air.

When I smoke joints on Sunday afternoon in my apartment, I feel free. I made my body my own when it was the only home I had, and now this 650 square feet in Rosemont is my territory. I can smoke my medicines as I please and listen to my favourite Karen Dalton vinyl as many times as

I'd like. Damn, Karen was right when she said that it's so hard to tell who's going to love you best. The smoke disappears in the beams of sunlight like phantoms leaving an opaque haze in the air. I think about how, now that my mother is dead, her expectations of me dissipate as well. Now that my mom is gone, now that I can see nikâwiy for who she is and what she has the capacity to give, I have no one to blame for my shit but myself.

The last time I spoke to my mom, I was leaving Montreal on a train to Brooklyn. It was 9 a.m. my time, and 7 a.m. her time. Admittedly, I knew it was early. But I was inspired by new love and the glow it adds to the world. So inspired, I wanted to break the silence by dialing her number that morning. She had sleep in her voice, or medication perhaps, but she was happy. I told her that I was heading to New York with my new love, that I was okay. The sun was coming up over the horizon as the train barrelled through the industrial parts of the Southwest, illuminating the graffiti, tags on the concrete, and the sharp edges of the modernist architecture of newly built condos colonizing the neighbourhood. I remember turning my shoulder to look at nîcimôs, and he smiled. The air was just thick with love, and we wanted to share it with the world.

When I couldn't stay any longer in Edmonton, when all my haunts began haunting me,[1] I moved to Montreal. Montreal had long been the place I had run to, ever since visiting when I was sixteen. I was spending the summer in Trois-Rivières on a language program. More accurately, I was learning how to smoke French cigarettes, being introduced to Leonard Cohen and underage drinking in bars, and finding out how to swindle men twice my age. We hitched a ride with some of the older guys who were staying at the college where our language program was, and the grit of Montreal immediately resonated with me. The whole damn city, outside of the Old Port, was like the poorest parts of downtown Regina. Filth and debauchery positively radiated through the air after dark, and the Village was a mess of men in assless leather chaps and soft bois as far as the eye could gaze down Ste-Cats— finally, a space to match my wilding dreams. Sometimes I still get glimpses through my old eyes, when I drive past a dressed-up window, or an intersection that's particularly glittery in the night. Potential swells in my chest and I remember that feeling of having the whole world laid out in front of me, ready and ripe for my taking.

What is it about Montreal, that je ne sais quoi? Maybe it's in my blood. After all, they called us the Saulteaux because of our relationships to the French, and everyone knows how the Métis got down. Montreal, you're like the drunk freaky cousin to its older imperialist brother. Montreal, you're so nouveau riche, good for a cheap thrill.[2] I know it's sin to love the city you're in, as a so-called ~displaced N.D.N.~ but Montreal, I love you. nîcimos, I love you.

nîcimos is good for a cheap thrill, too, like this city he grew up in. A city he reps with that thirst trap, French inhale he sports. Once nîcimos asked me why I think he has a commercial smell, like The Bay and freshly cleaned hotel rooms. I replied, "Because they remind me of my mother."

The day my mom died, nîcimos was there. Where there's a will, there's a babe. We were at a queer music festival called Idapalooza, which is probably better described as a queer orgy that takes place on a commune in the Tennessee mountains. The commune was on a plot of land gifted to the current residents by an affluent queer ancestor for the queer resistance. The queers who lived there year-round called it Ida. There was no cell service, just a spotty internet telephone for emergencies. When the organizers recited the names of my family members over the speaker at daily announcements, some part of me already knew.

"I didn't want to say the name they gave in case it wasn't your preferred name," the administrator for the festival said when I reached the commune's office. "Thank you, thank you, thank you," I said (I think). But in true millennial form, I couldn't remember anyone's number off by heart, except my dad's cellphone because I'd been dialing it in emergencies for a decade now. When my wallet would get pickpocketed in a random city, or if I had bottomed out in yet a different city with no job and was calling to beg for $50, my pride nowhere to be seen. My dad didn't answer, though.

The commune had parking at another location. We had dropped off our car in a field, and then got picked up in the commune's truck, which was always driven by some yt butch. I rushed out of the office, passed a couple fucking in the hammock. Bits of flesh protruding out the holes caught my eye as I made my way back to the whore-tex where we had unwittingly set up the tent after arriving in the middle of the night. We had set up hastily after getting lost in the backroads and seeing a few too many mean-looking rednecks while trying to find this paradise. We were just grateful to set up camp in any place we could. We should have known from the moaning we heard coming from the woods, but we passed out instantly, only to find the next morning that we were there, in a constant orgy including kiddie pools, lube wrestling, lots of glittery costumes, and spanking stations.

I found nîcimos asleep in our tent, and a wave of guilt washed over me for waking him from this paradise. We had just been bathing naked in the river with our friends earlier in the day, unashamed, our genitals to the wind even if our genders didn't match the colonial-western institutional and medicalized reading of bodies, and so full of love. And now an unsettling force was creeping in at the edges of this bubble we had created for ourselves, infringing on the ceremonies we had been undertaking on this piece of land that had been passed down from generation to generation of queers, albeit a complicated prayer. Rural queers had run to Ida for decades now, to the land our queer ancestors had sworn to make an Adam and Eve-esque paradise for their queer descendants, forever. Having fed our heads, sweaty body to sweaty body, spirits dancing into the night: this is how we pray.

The trans porn star who drove us back to our car could see me getting increasingly distressed. I'll admit, I was on the verge of a panic attack. But I kept refusing the kind offer to use his phone. "No thank you, no thank you, no thank you," I said (I think).

When he extended his hand to me, holding his cell phone, a final time, I looked up at his face, and it was kind. I forgot we were all family here. I was still falling back on my tried and true self-protective ways. My fuck you wall. My I-can-do-anything-and-get-anything-all-by-myself, so-I-don't-need-you attitude. My thick skin and my impenetrable don't-mess-with-me public face. All of which were qualities I probably learned from my mom, and from surviving that house.

I took the porn star's phone and dialled my dad one more time. This time, my brother picked up.

"Hello?"

"B, it's ... your sibling."

"Where are you? We've been trying to get a hold of you for days. We sent a cop to your house, you know."

"The cops?! What the f— ... Look, can you just tell me what's going on?"

There was a long pause before B managed, "Mom's dead. She had a cardiac arrest last night after an ulcer bled out too much in her stomach. Because she lost blood, they did CPR but the air wasn't getting to her brain. She's brain dead, Lindsay. She's gone."

That's how I found out my mom had died. Cruising through the Tennessee mountains talking on a phone graciously lent to me by someone I had jacked off to.

There was no time left to sort through the pain together, or anything other than one-sided closure. You're not meant to speak ill of the dead. All I have left is humility. Things my mom left for me: A profound respect for years of emotional labour she undertook, which I hardly even recognized or saw. The ability to begin separating peoples' entitlement to, expectations of, and projections of me from what I want and who I am. The ability to cultivate an environment that nurtures and makes space for only the most divine. A newfound respect for the care she laboured over day in and day out, which I didn't know yet, but would inherit upon her death. An understanding of the care she expressed to us through the home she kept, values I'll now pass on to my children.

When I fell in love nîcimos, I made a home for them by filling a bachelor apartment with all the tender things my mom used to show her care for me. In her absence, I would chase the feeling of her: satsuma bath products that filled the house with warmth when used, beef stew with dumplings, profiteroles, and bleached towels and sheets. While conceived differently and probably looking alternative to hers, it will be a family nonetheless. Every day, I am living the queer Indigenous future I used to think I'd never have, that I wasn't worthy of. I survived an apocalypse of NDN love, life after NDN love, and exceeded the limits of its loveless pretension, to breathe, fight, and fuck the Indigenous future, right here, right now, in this moment. As I've seen printed at the queer book fairs I frequented in my twenties, I am my ancestors' wildest dream.

I remember when we were driving up to Ida when the Nitty Scott song came on and brought me to tears: *Kiss your grandmother, and your mother too. 'Cause it's love for you that make 'em want to smother you.*[3] I didn't know that I would never get the chance to say any of this to her.

We've come full circle, haven't we, dear reader, recreated the cyclical rhythm of creation. Love as delicately as you'd burn sage. Love as ceremony. Love hard because that is where your dominion lies.

ACKNOWLEDGEMENTS

I've got to give the first shout-out to my partner, Seb, for all the rides to and from events, back rubs, emotional support, and late-night Red Bull runs. His support makes my goals realizable. Everything I have would be meaningless if he weren't here to share it with.

So much gratitude to my parents and siblings, the whole complex web. They loved me into the person I am today.

Shout-out to my dearest, longest friend, Sasha, who has seen me through so many different versions of myself. She loved me before anyone cared about my fat ass. That's the tastemaker in her. The story of me will forever be intertwined with the story of her. She is my longest love.

Thanks to Leanne who did an early reading of my manuscript, whose edits (gently) make me a better writer, and who is fiercely supportive of the vision of young Indigenous writers. That untie power is who I'm tryna be.

Thanks to Robyn, who took time out of her schedule of being the coolest parent ever, doing a PhD, and fucking with the state on the daily, to do an early read on this manuscript. I'm so proud of the community work we've done together, and all the community we've created.

Billy touched me with the generosity of his blurb, and trust, considering that I gave him my manuscript so late. So much love for my whole Cree mean girl squad: Billy and Emily (kookum and mooshum).

My NDN girl posse. We might not all be girls anymore, but we'll be kin for life. I got a whole book of stories brewing about my main bitches in the struggle, Molly and Brandi.

To Dayna for taking the cover image for this book and for always having my back. Thanks for driving with me to Kahnawake in the dead of winter to get this shot. Thanks for being dope kin, generally.

I'm ever grateful to Chelsea, who did the Plains Cree editing on this and who was the first person to teach me Plains Cree, and kinship, outside of a few city kid words.

A lot of NDN art love went into the book, too. I'm ever grateful for all the artists making smart work that speaks to and for NDN bb grrrls, many of whom I referenced herein, such as Lacie Burning and Thirza Cuthand, but others who weren't mentioned with whom I've been lucky to build collaborative kinships, such as Fallon Simard.

Special shout-outs go to Mad Aunty for the custom necklace work from the cover, Savage Rose for the most gorgeous pair of earrings I've ever owned, also on the cover, and to Kablusiak for illustrating portions of this book. I am so grateful for all the artists who let me think alongside their work.

Thank you to the Black community in Montreal and Toronto, and all my Black kin, who took the time to discuss instances of AAVE in earlier printings of this book. I am always learning and I am ever grateful for your generosity, kindness, and kinship.

I'm not sure I can continue these acknowledgements without it becoming a tangled mess of peoples and places that span over a decade of my life. I'm sure I'm forgetting folks. So perhaps I will simply end by saying thank you, a hundred times over, for every person in all the constellations of people who touched me during the periods outlined within this book and during its writing. Thank Creator for all the love I've been granted in this life. Hashtag blessed.

NOTES

*Initials and pseudonyms are used throughout the book to protect the privacy of the characters in the story.

Love Story Medicine

1. Kim Anderson, *Life Stages of Native Women.*
2. Audra Simpson, "Making Native Love" (on www.cyberpowwow.net).
3. Cher, "Do You Believe in Life after Love."
4. Kenny Rogers and Dolly Parton, "Islands in the Stream."
5. Kim Tallbear, *Future Imaginary Dialogues* (on vimeo.com)
6. eyos, "NDN Weather Report," *GUTS.*
7. See Gerald Vizenor's writing about warriors of survivance.
8. See Joshua Whitehead's spelling of this colloquialism in *Jonny Appleseed.*
9. Drake, "Underground Kings."
10. Judith Butler, *Gender Trouble.*
11. Michael Hardt and Antonio Negri, "*De Singularitate* 1: Of Love Possessed," *Commonwealth.*
12. See the Dominion Lands Act system of 1871.
13. Sinclair Ross, "The Painted Door."
14. Molly Swain of the podcast *Métis in Space* has named it this. Indigenous Peoples are using our own technological traditions—our worldviews, our languages, our stories, and our kinship—as guiding principles in imagining possible futures for ourselves and our communities.
15. Missy Elliot, "Work It."
16. *Mysterious Skin.*

Toxic Masculinities

1. Cat Power, "Lived in Bars."
2. Feist, "Feel It All."
3. Elton John, "Honky Cat."
4. Michael Hardt and Antonio Negri, "De Singularitate 1: Of Love Possessed," *Commonwealth.*

5. Katy Perry, "I Kissed a Girl."
6. EMA, "Marked."
7. Charles Bukowski, "Oh Yes," *War All the Time.*
8. Leanne Simpson, *Dancing on Our Turtle's Back.*
9. Lykke Li, "Sadness Is a Blessing."

The Prairie Wind Is Gay Af

1. W. O. Mitchell, *Who Has Seen the Wind.*
2. Love Inc., "Broken Bones."
3. Arcade Fire, "Sprawl II."
4. *The Rocky Horror Picture Show.*
5. *Rent.*

Queerness

1. Joan Jett, "Crimson and Clover."
2. "Boundaries," *Chai Chats Podcast* (on Soundcloud.com).
3. The Gossip, "Standing in the Way of Control."
4. A reference to the 2001 film and graphic novel *Ghost World*—but probably mostly the film.

Vision 4: wâkâyôs

1. A reference to a recorded statement by Dylan Campbell Scott, wherein he described sending children to residential schools in order to eradicate Indigenous Peoples (a.k.a. The Indian Question).

Creation Story

1. Modest Mouse, "World at Large."
2. A reference to the show *Daria.*
3. HIM, "Join Me in Death."
4. MIA, "Galang."

The Spatiality of Yt Gays

1. See Sherene Razack's theory about spatiality.
2. A reference to something my friend Robyn Maynard said to me once.

3. See Judith Butler's theory about queer "self-making."
4. *Moulin Rouge*.

Queen City Punk

1. Wheatus, "Teenage Dirtbag."
2. "America Is the Terrorist" was a phrase that appeared on T-shirts for the Regina metal band Dirtbred.
3. Throwdown, "Forever."
4. Hatebreed, "Live for This."
5. Michelle Tea, *Rent Girl*.
6. Metric, "Combat Baby."

wîhtikow

1. Chrystos, *Not Vanishing*.

BRB B2B: All the Places We Called Home, Then Burned

1. Feist, "Let It Die."
2. Fleetwood Mac, "Dreams."
3. Tegan and Sara, "Call It Off."
4. A reference to a character and a story within the fictitious world of the television series *The L Word*.
5. A reference to the opening title track for *The L Word*.
6. The Kills, "Pots and Pans."
7. Cat Power, "Ramblin' (Wo)man."
8. Mirah, "Archipelago."
9. The Yeah Yeah Yeahs, "Zero."
10. Jenny Lewis and the Watson Twins, "You Are What You Love."
11. *Fair Play*.
12. Sleigh Bells, "Rill Rill."
13. Joni Mitchell, "California."
14. Giant Drag, "This Isn't It."
15. Drake, "Over."
16. Amy Winehouse, "Tears Dry on Their Own."
17. Stars, "Your Ex-Lover Is Dead."

Vision 8: pihpihcêw

1. A reference to a series by Amy Malbeuf and Jordan Bennett, inspired by a Twitter hashtag under the same name.
2. Audre Lorde, *A Burst of Light*.

OG (Kush)

1. See Truman Capote's *Breakfast at Tiffany's*.

Feminine Divine

1. Sleater-Kinney, "Modern Girl."

Prayer 9: For My NDN Bb Girls

1. Chrystos, *Not Vanishing*.
2. Missy Elliott, "Work It."
3. See Tupac's poetry collection *The Rose That Grew from Concrete*.

For My Descendants

1. Kimya Dawson, "Loose Lips."

What Artists Have Taught Me

1. *RuPaul's Drag Race* All Star Season 3.
2. Janelle Monae, "Crazy, Classic, Life."

Epilogue (Tio'tia:ke)

1. St. Vincent, "Laughing with a Mouth of Blood."
2. Sia, "Cheap Thrills."
3. Nitty Scott, "Little Sister."

ABOUT THE AUTHOR

Lindsay Nixon is a Toronto-based Cree-Métis-Saulteaux SSHRC doctoral scholarship recipient, a McGill University Art History Ph.D. candidate, and an assistant professor in Ryerson University's Department of English. They previously held the position of Editor-at-Large for *Canadian Art*, served as the Arts and Literary Summit programmer for MagNet 2019, and edited *mâmawi-âcimowak*, an independent art, art criticism, and literature journal. Their writing has appeared in *The Walrus, Malahat Review, Room, GUTS, esse, Teen Vogue, CV2/Prairie Fire, The New Inquiry* and other publications.

ALSO AVAILABLE FROM METONYMY PRESS:

Dear Black Girls
Shanice Nicole and Kezna Dalz

ZOM-FAM
Kama La Mackerel

Dear Twin
Addie Tsai

Little Blue Encyclopedia (for Vivian)
Hazel Jane Plante

Lyric Sexology Vol. 1
Trish Salah

Fierce Femmes and Notorious Liars:
A Dangerous Trans Girl's Confabulous Memoir
Kai Cheng Thom

Small Beauty
jiaqing wilson-yang

She Is Sitting in the Night: Re-visioning Thea's Tarot
Oliver Pickle